TREE LEAVES
BREAKING THE FALL OF THE LOUD SILENCE

ROSENNA BAKARI

KARIBU PUBLISHING

CONTENTS

Foreword — v
Preface — vii
Join the movement — ix
Introduction — xi

1. 1: When the Journey Begins — 1
2. 2: Present Perfect — 18
3. 3: In Your Skin — 34
4. 4: Family Affairs — 50
5. 5: Shoes on the Wrong Feet — 65
6. 6: Fetal Position — 80
7. 7: Fairy Tells — 95
8. 8: Pandora's Box — 109
9. 9: Guinea Pig Learns To Speak — 126
10. 10: The Day After Tomorrow — 142
11. 11: I Am — 158
12. 12: The Knock at the Door — 174

About the Author — 191
Blank — 195

Trees Leaves: Breaking the Fall of the Loud Silence

Copyright © 2016 by Rosenna Bakari

Printed in the United States of America. All rights reserved. No part of this book may be reproduced or transmitted in any form or by any means without written permission from the author.

First edition

ISBN 978-0-9971699-0-4

Karibu Publishing

To contact author:

rosennab@talkingtreessurvivors.com

Website: http:/www.Talkingtreessurvivors.com

FOREWORD

Consider this book a search light, a light tower, a buoy for survivors of childhood sexual abuse around the world. I have heard your silent call. You have heard mine. We are not alone. Together we can grow into making meaning of our lives, despite the trauma, rather than remain socially and emotionally haunted by it.

There are over 50 million survivors of childhood sexual abuse in the United States. Half of us never tell, never talk about it, and never begin the healing process. Keeping secrets, protecting families and living in shame are obstacles that hinder us from healing. Over time, living openly knocks down many of these obstacles, but not without support.

This book is consistent with the mission of Talking Trees, Inc. which is to support solid concepts about healing. The goals are to create a language to address experiences, promote an understanding of healing based on human development, clarify treatment options, and encourage a commitment to healing as a lifelong and wholistic journey. I am thankful that this book has found you on your journey.

PREFACE

I had traveled to four continents in three months and was on the way back to the United States. There was only a week left of the *Semester at Sea* voyage. Naturally, my thoughts turned toward my regular activities at home. I realized how much I missed being active in the *Talking Trees* online community I created to empower survivors five years ago. I had worked out a system to schedule my daily posts so my presence could still be felt when I had no online access. However, I found myself feeling the absence of community. I felt eager to close the distance. As I stood over the rail on deck eight of the World Odyssey, looking out into the ocean in hopes of sighting a whale, I longed for a connection to adult survivors of childhood sexual abuse. No whale showed, but a whale of an idea did appear. I should end this journey by putting together the manuscript of *Talking Trees* posts. The community members had made many requests for such a book.

The following 366 pointers represent a selection of the daily *Talking Trees* posts that I have written over a period of five years. I do not consider them affirmations because affirmations make people feel good. While some of these posts will make survivors feel good, others are intended to challenge the survivor to see

PREFACE

themselves differently. When we are challenged to see the world differently our sense of comfort may become disturbed. So, I beckon readers to watch their reactions, especially if you read a statement or pointer that makes you uncomfortable. See if you can make sense of it in a way that motivates you instead of frustrates you.

There is no order to the writings. They are dated for convenience, not for purpose. Some days you may only have time to read a short post. Some days you may want to read several posts. However the pointers can be used to support your healing is how you should use them.

JOIN THE MOVEMENT

Breaking the silence of childhood sexual abuse is not a task. It is a journey of healing, a lifestyle of authenticity and a commitment to move humanity forward. You do not need to be a survivor of childhood sexual abuse to help us break the silence. You need only to create safe space for others to find their voice and design their path. You can help by doing any or all of the following:

- Spread the word about this book. Each book sold represents a voice that is tired of living in silence.
- Leave a review of the book on whatever media you can access online or offline.
- Follow "Talking Trees Adult Survivors of CSA" on Facebook.
- Go to Talkingtreessurvivors.com and sign up for the monthly newsletter.
- Go to RosennaBakari.com and sign up for updates of forthcoming titles and other author activities.
- Learn about "bodily autonomy" and "gene pooling." Writings about these concepts and theories can be found on my author page. They help frame the world

epidemic of sexual abuse to move from the individual to the collective, where there is safer space to heal.
- Invite Dr. Rosenna Bakari as a professional speaker to your campus, company, or conference.
- Heal one day at a time.

INTRODUCTION

INVISIBLE VICTIM

I am an invisible victim of an invisible crime. It is a crime that a mother cannot face, a wife refuses to face and the justice system is not equipped to face. It is a crime society is too afraid to face. I am a victim of incest and childhood sexual abuse. There is no police record, no family outcry, nor neighborly support, because by the time I could speak of it, nobody cared.

Nobody cared about the approaching 30-years-old therapist having post-traumatic flashbacks of rape at age seven. Nobody understood the shame of being molested for two years during high school. Nobody understood me wanting to take my life over a coerced sexual relationship at age eighteen. Even my mind betrayed me by repressing memories and leaving only boogie-man images and dark traces of violation. My body filled in the gaps with fainting spells, fibroids, seizures, arthritis, gray hair at the age of 21, and even a pinhole in my heart. My body remembers what my mind forgot.

Now, I fight back with my 3rd-degree black belt in Taekwondo. When I cannot fight, I run marathon miles. I strengthen my heart in the weight room, and I dance to remind myself that my body is now free. I have calculated that it takes approximately

INTRODUCTION

ten hours a week of intense exercise to manage my post-traumatic stress. My solace is knowing that I am not alone.

There are approximately 50 million survivors of childhood sexual abuse in America. More than half of them have never told a soul. Most survivors who disclose are not supported in their healing by their families. Some survivors who tell will not be believed. Some of them will be believed and told to just get over it. Some will even be blamed for the abuse. Some survivors, like me, will be directly requested to keep quiet to support the family.

How the family looks is far more important than how individuals in the family feel. Rarely is the choice made to create safe space for the survivor. The survivor is left to figure out how to create physical distance between themselves and the violators because they remain part of a shared environment. Rarely is the violator admonished for his or her actions, much less brought to justice. The invisible victims are left to their internal mechanisms to sort through the trauma.

What I can tell you about being an invisible victim is that you live with a profound sense of insignificance. The question looms over you for a lifetime, "When will someone love me enough to acknowledge my experience and my pain?" Each sacrifice you make to be in the company of those who ignore your pain, you feel smaller and smaller. You have no idea what it feels like to matter in the world, because when your pain is so big, and you are told to ignore it, the only way you can do that is to make yourself small. You get to the point where you feel like if you have to be that small, you might as well not be here at all. Many survivors live with thoughts of suicide on a daily basis.

In 2010, I began a mission to find the estimated 40 million survivors (at that time) of incest and childhood sexual abuse, not because I wanted to help them, but because I needed them to help me. My hope was that they could console me, affirm for me my pain, or teach me how to let it go. I wanted to find those millions of people who live with horrors like mine, horrors of a stolen childhood. But what I found was a loud silence. To my disappointment, my outreach efforts (theatrical performances, conferences, and social media platforms) barely yielded thousands, not millions, of echoes of healing. Increasingly, individuals would email me, stop by my office, or whisper to me in public that they too are a survivor. When I asked why they do not participate in the events for survivors, I heard the silence. "My family does not know." "I do not want my friends on social media to know that I am a survivor, so I cannot post." "I feel responsible for what happened." "My spouse does not know." "I do not want to be labeled as a survivor." These are the same reasons survivors do not seek therapy. So, my next step was to figure out where survivors were hiding their pain.

I had to resort to the research journals to find the answer to satisfy my curiosity. What I found was that many adult survivors of childhood sexual abuse and incest are taking their silent pain to prison; others are taking it to the physician, and still more are taking their pain to the drug rehab center. All of these places are over-represented by survivors.

My pain led me to the physician. On the auspicious date of 12/12/12, just one month after my 50th birthday, I had a total abdominal hysterectomy to remove what my doctor told me was "an angry uterus." I thought, she has no idea how angry it is. But I was not willing to go to the rehab center or prison to further reveal my pain, and I do not believe that other survivors should either. I am also tired of going to the physician.

On a more positive note, I found that over the last twenty years, cases of child sexual abuse have declined. Society has done a significant job with prevention of child sex abuse by calling on communities and families to take responsibility. Professional advocates told communities what to look for, what to do, what to say and who to tell so that children can be protected. Unfortunately, we have not begun to expand those resources and concerns into healing tools when prevention fails, and it does fail.

INTRODUCTION

We still lose the fight for one out of six girls and one out of eight boys.

When prevention fails, we put our heads under the pillow and sweep the problem under the rug. Society is afraid to acknowledge its dysfunction, afraid to admit its failure. It hides its cultural shame. Adult survivors of childhood sexual abuse and incest are abandoned in the healing process. Less than 20% of child victims are identifies, leaving behind 80% of victims that will enter adulthood with anyone saying as much as "sorry."

So, each day I wake up I realize that there is work to be done. I have managed a website and Facebook, page since 2010, Talking Trees: Adult Survivors of CSA. Each year I organize a Safe Space Day Conference on April 15 to celebrate the resilience of adult survivors. I have also published a series of informational videos online. In 2014 Talking Trees Inc. became a tax-exempt, nonprofit organization with me serving as Executive Director and Founder. The purpose of the organization is to continue to create healing resources, such as this book.

It is important to recognize that not all survivors have the same experience. The invasiveness of the physical contact is related to the degree of trauma. For example, penetration is more invasive than fondling a child's body and that difference is typically reflected in the degree of trauma. Survivors who were subjected to the most invasive trauma are more likely to develop post-traumatic stress symptoms. The grooming method, the process in which perpetrators prepare victims for a response of silence through manipulation, is related to the degree of guilt and shame a survivor carries. Some survivors were violently raped rather than groomed while others were groomed for months or years before the first touch. Groomed victims tend to suffer more from negative self-talk.

The frequency of violation and the number of violators before the age of eighteen are important factors. The frequency of contact between the violator and victim may influence the self-image of adult survivors. Many survivors shared a home with the violators while some survivors may have had infrequent contact. Some survivors experienced a single event of abuse by one violator while many survivors experienced years of abuse by a series of violators or simultaneous violators. The age of violation might influence repressed memory if the survivor was too young to process the experience. Older survivors may experience extreme guilt and responsibility for the abuse. These are all basic factors that do not take into account the current mental capacity, environmental resources and support of the survivor. Hopefully, one can appreciate that there is no set path for healing. There is no one size fits all. And we have to be extremely careful not to judge where we or others are in the healing journey. Every survivor must carve out their personal healing path.

Nevertheless, the nature of the trauma itself has been identified. We are healing from the body snatchers that left us numb, disconnected and over or under protective of ourselves. We are healing from the mind-blowers that left us psychologically weakened with negativity and distortions about ourselves and the world. We are healing from the heartbreakers that forced us into perpetual emotional defense. And we accept the identity of "adult survivor of childhood sexual abuse" to help us frame the experience so that we can work through all of these issues that affect us collectively. The identity assures us that we are not alone in our struggle with guilt and shame, difficulty with relationships, triggers, loss of family, and that perpetual feeling of not being enough. We recognize our right to heal because we know that that there is a better way of being in the world than what we experienced. We are no longer choosing invisibility over ugly truths.

INTRODUCTION

I'm Tired

I'm tired of living with the will to die
I'm tired of people telling me I should not cry
I'm tired of having to make myself so small
I'm tired of living with my back against the wall
I'm tired of feeling permanently stuck
I'm tired of feeling like I want to give up
Now, what's this I hear about a talking tree?
Something about branches that can speak to me
Saying I do not have to take this pain to my grave
Telling me how to constructively release my rage
So many lost souls are simply hidden in this tree
Each branch I touch whispers "here, we are free."

1: WHEN THE JOURNEY BEGINS

We do not need the world to validate us, adapt to us, or change so that we can heal. When we begin to heal, the world around us will change. Your personal healing is not about the world. It is about you and your response to the world. Peace is internal.

January 1

Sexual abuse is a part of our sexual history. Living openly is not an invitation for people to cross boundaries of privacy, and we are certainly not obligated to disclose any more than we feel comfortable. If you tell someone that you dated a famous person you don't have to state the level of intimacy you shared with that person. The purpose of living openly is to find your voice and heal. If you live openly without creating boundaries, then you will likely not find your voice and likely not heal. Creating boundaries is part of the work even though the boundaries change. Every aspect of the healing journey must be personally designed by the survivor. The more conscious the intention of your choices, the more likely you are to have a positive outcome that moves you forward.

January 2

"I cannot take this anymore." This sentiment can spark pivotal change in the survivor. You cannot take the hiding anymore, the pretending to be OK, the denial of the abuse, the praise of violators by those who still love and respect them despite knowing what they have done to you. This is a heavy burden to bear. Most survivors bear this burden well into their forties before they decide "I cannot take this life anymore." So, when you get here, know that you are at a turning point that will finally lead you to peace if you follow the path.

January 3

"Grooming" is a manipulative manner of creating a bond with a child to assure that the child will not disclose sexual abuse to anyone. That bond may be created by fear or admiration toward the perpetrator. Many adult survivors live in turmoil because they believe that they were responsible for the abuse. The guilt and shame that we experienced are exactly what the violator planted in our brains through grooming to assure our silence. Often, when fear is used, the violator convinces the child that they will not be believed, or that something terrible will happen if they tell. Often the violator will engage the child in a forbidden act, such as drug use, watching pornography, stealing or even a privilege as simple as staying up past bedtime. The violator may promise to keep the secret for the child, which initiates the bond. Later, this secret is used as the threat against the child to not tell once the violator begins to touch the child. The child does not have to be threatened directly either. The child, likely in a dysfunctional family, already "knows" that they will be blamed and punished for their misdeeds if the violator does not keep their secret. The violator traps the child by turning the secret around. All this becomes mixed up in the child's mind. The child's mind is not developed enough to sort out the complexity of their misbehavior, the violator's original intent, and the dysfunctional family dynamics. Silence is the most reasonable survival choice from the perspective of the child. Meanwhile the intent to sexually abuse the child was likely in the mind of the violator for a long time before the child felt any discomfort or concern. The violator creates the path and leads the child down it. The child's mind, unfortunately, continues to develop according to the path set by the violator. The child grows up with the violator's scripts still playing in the adult survivor's head. Healing is necessary for adult survivors to find the life path we were meant to travel.

January 4

That terrible urge we sometimes have to not want to live anymore is a calling. The will to die may be a calling. It is not a calling for your physical death, but for your psychological rebirth. To heal, we have to let a lot of ourselves die. We have to let the expectations of loved ones to accept or understand us die. We have to let the desire to be saved die but we do not have to die just because no one will save us. We have to let our dysfunctional beliefs die. All that does not serve us in our healing dies as we heal. We have spent so much time feeding the dysfunction that we exhaust ourselves of our will to live. You do not have to die a physical death; you just have to renew your mind.

January 5

The problem with sex for too many survivors is that we have never done it right. Many survivors have never grown into a loving relationship that developed into a sexual relationship through desire. Many survivors only experience sex as an obligation. Obligatory sex is not a turn-on, not fun, not exciting and not desirable. No one is obligated to have sex with anyone. Furthermore, sex is not an activity or favor you do "for" someone or "to" someone. Sex is a close contact experience of physical pleasure that you "share" with someone. Survivors who have been introduced to sexuality from a grossly distorted perspective may choose partners that mimic the selfish demands of violators. So healing must include sexual health as well as our mental and physical health. No more victim sex.

January 6

The healing journey is a concept, not a physical destination. So be weary of anyone trying to lead you to the "Promised Land." Sometimes we want the pain to stop so badly that we swallow whatever pill anyone offers us. Sometimes we want to silence the voices in our head so much that we listen to whatever someone else spouts out of their mouth. Sometimes we want to be saved so badly that we seek refuge in whatever place someone drags us. No matter how well intentioned they are, people, books, therapy, and programs can only offer us pointers on the healing path. They may temporarily quench the thirst of a panting traveler, or cheer us on with a smile. However, each day it is you who must do the walking, and you who must have the strength to pass those making promises they cannot keep. No one can make the path easier for you to walk, except to walk it with you. Even then, you may part at the fork in the road. You must keep traveling your path, with your own two feet and conscious mind.

January 7

There are over 50 million adult survivors of childhood sexual abuse in America. That is an epidemic, and arguably, a mental health crisis. Half of survivors never tell anyone. However, that still leaves 25 million survivors who have disclosed. Yet, public conversation about adult survivors of childhood sexual abuse is still absent. Why? Because there is a big difference between sharing a secret and living openly. Living openly is a concept that has been largely forwarded by Talking Trees, Inc. The goal is to create forums and dialogues that lend themselves to awareness and understanding of the issues that face survivors of childhood sexual abuse. The emphasis is on survivors' pain and process for healing rather than the victimization. Living openly is not a repetitive monologue to test people's tolerance for disclosure. Living openly is advocacy, not staying silent when speaking can raise awareness.

January 8

The healing journey is so challenging because you never know when you are going to run out of gas. We could be doing just fine until the smallest unexpected situation comes along and shakes us. It could be a visit from a relative, a child leaving home, a consensual sexual encounter, a marriage proposal or any other everyday event. Any event may trigger us and bring our experience of abuse to the foreground of our lives. We may begin to doubt ourselves, feel abandoned or resort to old patterns of victimization. However, the more entrenched you are in healing, the less time it takes you to refuel.

January 9

Sometimes we try too hard. It is harder to control other people than it is to control ourselves. It is harder to hold on to a failing relationship than it is to let it go. It is harder to stick to your rules and expectations that open the door to pain than it is to let change flow into your life. It is harder to be on guard waiting for someone to hurt you than it is to trust yourself to make good decisions. The harder patterns may be more familiar, or may be all that you know how to do. So you may cling to them. But healing makes life easier.

January 10

Feelings are important to the degree that they help us look "within." When we use our feelings to make judgments about others and the world based on our level of comfort, we live within illusions rather than growth. The illusions happen whether we use our feelings to make negative or positive judgments about others for the sake of categorizing them into our lives. If we judge actions that make us feel good as right and actions that make us feel bad as wrong, we may fail to see people and experiences for what they are. All we may see is a reflection of our reality, which may not be an accurate interpretation of any particular experience. But if we use all of our feelings to go within, explore our minds and take responsibility for our peace, then growth will be continuous.

January 11

There are some small, but significant, tasks that we can do to put us in a different mindset as we approach the world each day. We know that we should live differently but may think that we need to make big changes in our lives. Sometimes the little changes that we make can lead to big differences in the way we see the world. These are some suggestions that can open you up to new possibilities: 1) Make your bed each morning before you leave the house. 2) Open at least one window in your house at least once a week for a short period even in the dead of winter. 3) Go to a social event at least once a month. 4) If there are no social events that interest you, create one by inviting a friend to do for a social outing. 5) Skip church one Sunday to sleep in late and know that God will meet you exactly where you are because God is within you. 6) Intentionally quiet your space by turning off the TVs, and music, computers, and cell phone for at least 30 minutes a day while you read, cook, clean, meditate, or just relax. 7) Always greet the people who service you, cashiers, waiters, repairmen and bus drivers included. 8) Listen to a spiritual book on tape. 8) Write a poem instead of journaling. 9) Tell your children you love them. 10) Practice offering compliments to people around you each day. These actions may seem unimportant, but healing sometimes requires us to make the seemingly unimportant important and the seemingly important unimportant.

January 12

When we break the silence, there is usually some external backlash. Family members become angry or distant. Co-workers may ignore you; relationships may become strained. But none of the external consequences are as scary as the internal resistance that we can get. The brain will fight itself. Dreams may become nightmares. Depression may flare up. Anxiety may manifest. Physical illness or irritation may occur. Internal resistance to breaking the silence is common. The stronger the defenses you created to survive, the more internal resistance you may experience when you break your silence. Try to remember and appreciate that the internal discomfort is part of healing. You are allowing yourself to expose what has been hidden in you a long time. It is all coming up to be healed. You do not need control the junk that comes up if you "watch it." Allow the pain and you will avoid further suffering.

January 13

Healing is a commitment to oneself, and it is a benefit to the world. The commitment is to live in truth and to love yourself, even when the truth is ugly or uncomfortable. Because the truth will set you free. It sets you free because it takes less energy and resources to live without hiding, to live unapologetically, and to live authentically and transparently. You reach out with the energy you once used to hide and isolate. The energy you once used resisting, you can use to love. The resources you once used to cover up your pain you can now use to move humanity forward. Once you are free, the world is one step closer to being free.

JANUARY 14

There are ordinary, wise and caring people in the world who can facilitate the healing of survivors. The challenge is that survivors who are in the most turmoil may have the greatest difficulty attracting these people into their lives. As you engage in the healing work, you will begin to attract people into your life who can support you. But that does not mean that they will stay or that you will feel better while they are there. It only means that they may be able to listen and reflect back to you who and how you are presenting to the world. "Relationships are not here to make us happy. They are here to make us conscious" (*The Power of Now*, Eckhart Tolle). At least, that is how it goes on the healing path. The more we allow relationships to bring consciousness into our life, rather than more bitterness, anger and resentment, the more we will heal.

JANUARY 15

There is the assumption that survivors should be ready to move on since the abuse happened so long ago. However, the reality for many survivors is that the longer they live without addressing the abuse, the worse the effects may become. Many survivors deal better with the abuse early into adulthood and convince themselves that life is fine. However, as we age in life and understand more about the world our distortions unravel and result in confusion about ourselves and our world. We instinctively feel a need to bring our past into our present to explore and resolve what went wrong. We are in search of our true selves, not the self that evolved out of the need to respond to dysfunction and abuse.

January 16

The term "dissonance" conveys the feeling that we have when our thoughts, feelings, and actions are not aligned. The incongruence creates psychological unease. The unease may be conscious or unconscious. There are only three ways to resolve the dissonance. We can change our actions to be consistent with our thoughts. We can change our thoughts to be consistent with our actions. We can create a rationale for the contradiction between the thought and action and accept the dissonance. As a child, only the last two options are available to us since we cannot control the behavior demanded from us by the violator. So it is common to change our thoughts to match the behavior or to rationalize the behavior. Our minds do this to relieve the anxiety on the brain. Our brain may even allow us to "fall in love" with our violator so that the emotions are consistent with the actions that take place. The violator's grooming techniques may even be aimed at making the victim believe that falling in love is right to do. To the child, it is easier on the brain than resisting unwanted physical contact for months or years. Feeling love is a "logical" response to intimate contact. However, once victims grow up and grow out of their state of denial, they are often overwhelmed with guilt and shame. But the guilt and shame are not ours to carry. It belongs solely to the violators and those who support them. Our brains did the work to survive. We did whatever we knew to do to survive an experience that should never have been placed upon us. Now, as adults, we have a responsibility to continue healing.

January 17

Cognitive dissonance is the main reason grooming (preparing the victim for a response of secrecy) is so effective for violators. A child is not developmentally mature enough to sort out conflict and ambiguity. Children rely on the cues and guidance of adults and the environment. To respond to the psychological discomfort of being intimately touched, children yield to the demands of the environment for survival. Children in functional environments are likely to report discomfort to a trusting adult. However, in a dysfunctional environment where adults are not readily accessible for support, dissonance favors the perpetrator. The child is likely to resolve the dissonance by adopting the violator's script. As children age, they develop a better understanding of relationships and coping skills. Unfortunately, they still do not understand the role that cognitive dissonance played in their ability to adjust to living with the abuse. So they often begin to blame themselves. Cognitive dissonance helps us adapt to our environment by distorting reality. As we heal, we learn to live in truth. Cognitive dissonance may help you survive, but the truth will set you free.

January 18

Research shows that feelings, actions, and thoughts are connected. If you change one, the other two are likely to respond. Negative actions can lead to negative feelings. Negative thoughts can lead to negative actions. Negative feelings can lead to negative thoughts. The good news is that the opposite is true as well. Positive thoughts can lead to positive actions. Positive actions can lead to positive feelings. Positive feelings can lead to positive thoughts.

If we change just one of the mechanisms, we have a better chance of moving forward. So instead of trying to stop your negative thinking with more negative thinking, try stopping it with positive action instead. For example, if you are in a depressed mood take a walk or exercise instead of criticizing yourself. You should pay attention to all of the positive thoughts, actions, and feelings that you have access to so that you can pull them out of your "grab bag" when you need them.

JANUARY 19

Helping others is a great way to help ourselves, but only if we do not use service as a complete escape from our pain. If we attempt to help others instead of healing ourselves, then we do the world a disservice. Yes, facing our pain is more challenging than helping others face their pain, but the more we heal ourselves, the more effective we will be at helping others. When you become the light, everyone around you will become brighter, not just survivors, and the world will move forward. You do not need direct intervention in other people's lives to help the world. When you heal, you are having a direct impact on the world.

JANUARY 20

Survivors who choose no-contact for healing have likely eased into it. We've watched and waited as we healed. We waited until we were convinced that nothing would ever be any different with our families no matter what we did. Most survivors are in their 40s when we start to heal, so no-contact likely started after we had established some sort of support system and stability. We go no-contact to lean into the pain, not to stop it immediately. We often grow into no-contact as we grow out of victim mentality. We refuse contact with the violator first, then those who support them, then those who disapprove of us living openly. Maybe we start with no longer spending holidays with family and minimizing communication. There are a thousand scenarios that arise based on the survivor's need, not based on a presumed healing prescription. Talking Trees simply wants to support your desire to move forward in this direction because you have a right to be free. Still, you must design your own journey.

January 21

Healing is a natural process that we can facilitate or stifle with the adult decisions that we make now. However, the violators and those who supported them were already adults when they made the decisions to abuse or protect the abuser. They have already chosen their adult path and already given us their response to our abuse. They chose their path while we were children. So, they do not have any more choices to make. We are the ones who have to be brave enough to make the choices that set us free. Transformation is not transferable. We cannot transfer our transformation to our family who abused us. If they could not make the right choice when we were vulnerable children, it is highly unlikely that they will make the right choice for us as adults. So our commitment to healing cannot depend on the support we expect from our family of abuse.

January 22

Another complexity of incest and childhood sexual abuse is that trauma and dysfunction are interwoven. Trauma may include loss of a loved one, physical illness, accident or sudden negative change in life circumstances (such as due to divorce), as well as abuse. Most people emerge from trauma OK, especially when there is more than one person involved in the trauma since it has built-in support. But dysfunction is a lifestyle that gets seeded and embedded into a child's psyche and uses up the energy resources because the mind is in a constant state of threat. There are few resources for the mind to heal. With most survivors the trauma of sexual abuse is embedded within dysfunction. The physical experience of the abuse is kept secret by the dysfunction of the family, so there is no support for healing. Survivors sometimes get stuck in the healing process because they are focused on the physical aspect of the abuse rather than the dysfunction that kept it hidden. Refocus the healing on the dysfunction and you might be surprised at the progress you make.

January 23

Every day we heal more, even if we repeat a mistake or feel worse than before. We are always moving forward. We are always growing. We all have a certain number of mistakes we will make before we understand or before we change. So, even our mistakes count as progress. We have to not be hard on ourselves but know that we are the best we can be today. Our willingness to be thoughtful about our actions is enough. We do not need perfection. We are enough.

January 24

We should be careful not to turn our "experience" of abuse into "our story." The "story-telling" concept came from a model of "recovery", which I submit is different from a model of "healing," which has not been thoroughly constructed. The healing path is part of what we are creating; as we create space for healing, we are also creating the model. For thousands of years victims of sexual abuse have been silenced, so there was no healing path identified. That does not mean that we can take the model of recovery and apply it to healing. Wounds have to heal, and invariably leave scars. You recover from illness, such as a cold or even disease. We do not have a disease. We have wounds. Our wounds come from our experience of abuse, but the abuse is only a portion of who we are. The bigger our healing, the smaller the abuse becomes in our lives, over time, over lots of time. Of course, there are appropriate moments where sharing our "experience" is necessary for one reason or another. But that does not require us to create or commit to a story that becomes part of our identity. Healing is enough.

January 25

Age does not matter. Age does not make a victim of sexual abuse responsible in any way. People often judge survivors by what age they were when the abuse "ended," making the ignorant assumption that as a victim ages they will develop the power to stop the abuse. Sometimes victims develop enough strength to finally confront the perpetrator, but often there are too many environmental factors that prevent victims from acting on their own behalf. Sometimes the victim is so controlled by the perpetrator that the abuse lasts into the young adult years. Abuse also never leaves the victim in a "normal" state of mind. The emotional and mental capacity of the survivor is compromised, often to the degree that the "survivor" is easily targeted as a repeat victim. So a child who experienced sexual abuse at five may be re-victimized at age 15 by a different violator if the issues of sexual abuse were not adequately addressed. Age is not a factor in the ability to stop abuse, particularly incest, where children accumulate a lot of experience living as a victim. History of abuse, distortion of reality, instilled fear and manipulation are all factors that determine when the abuse stops, rather than age. Victims are just that… victims… until the abuse permanently stops.

January 26

We must be careful in our discussion about vulnerability to

childhood sexual abuse as if it is a virus. When we focus on child characteristics of vulnerability we take the focus off of violators. The reason children are sexually abused is because a violator sexually abused them, almost always a person known to them. Exposure to an abuser is the greatest vulnerability and predictor of childhood sexual abuse. We must start targeting violators for identification instead of victims. We must bring violators and their character to the light and give them less room to hide among the crowd as least likely suspects. We know too much to continue in denial. We know that parents, siblings, clergy, teachers, coaches, babysitters, neighbors and grandparents can be violators. Paying bills, having a charming personality or being in a relationship should not decrease suspicion. The number one problem that survivors encounter in healing is not being supported by family members. Too often the family chooses to focus on the problems caused by the survivor who wants to break the silence instead of the violator who committed the crime, thus perpetuating the problem.

January 27

The pain you feel with the memories is resistance trying to leave your body and brain. You have been living in a state of disbelief and with a lot of expectations that can never be met. These expectations are the ingredients for denial. "How could that have happened to me?" "Why would someone do that to me?" "How come I could not have a normal childhood?" "Why does my family not believe me?" "When will they choose me over the violator?" When memories of the abuse are attached to these questions, they will bring deep pain because we can never change the past. We have to live with acceptance. A horrible past has affected your present. You can change your present condition with acceptance of your past, not with resistance.

January 28

The sex life of survivors often developed by seeing themselves through the abuser's eyes. Many survivors have adopted patterns of sexual behavior from the violator. Survivors may seek sexual power from their partners because they are not yet ready to acknowledge when their power had been taken away. Some survivors have become fearful of sex because sensual pleasure evokes feelings of shame. Other survivors make themselves into a sexual sacrifice for a partner to use their body however they desire without seeking any pleasure in return. Restoring sexual health is an important part of healing. It includes the right to determine the level of sexual involvement, the right to use protection against disease as well as pregnancy and the right to expect orgasm for both you and your partner. Sexual health means that you do not allow yourself to be used as a human masturbation tool and that you do not use others that way as well.

January 29

In "error" to survive we grow up fast, faster than we can keep pace with ourselves. Instead of slowing down, we stress. Instead of asking for help, we become workaholics, instead of using our voice to speak about our pain, we use it to create pain in others by demanding and criticizing and scolding. Healing requires us to go back to practicing the innocence of childhood. We can practice laughing, trusting, not judging, and accepting people for who they are, including ourselves. Children seek fun in their lives. Children love to learn. Children allow others to take the lead sometimes. Now that you are an adult, feel free to be a child.

January 30

Accepting the title "adult survivors of childhood sexual abuse" helps us to identify with the experience so that we can work through the guilt and shame. The title also offers a collective understanding of dysfunctional patterns of thought and behavior that makes us feel less alone. But the title does not have to be a label for which we filter all of our experience forever. It can feel like being a survivor is the only experience in our lives that mattered or that mattered the most. However, we have had many experiences and many choices, some better than others. We can learn to respond to life out of other experiences.

JANUARY 31

When we feel like healing is too hard, we must call upon our strength, not our weakness. Instead of shutting down, we must open ourselves up to support. Instead of returning to the familiar patterns of survival, we must operate outside of our comfort zone. We seize the opportunity for growth. We go deeper into our resilience. We pursue the possibility of success with compassion for our mistakes.

2: PRESENT PERFECT

Since past experiences program us on a conscious, subconscious and unconscious level, it is critical to allow yourself to work through the pain of the past to live in the present.

FEBRUARY 1

There are victims who never quite find the healing path. They numb the pain through self-destructive behaviors that disrupt their lives and the lives of others. Society often discredits them and disregards the impact of the experience of abuse, as if the survivor caused the abuse by having bad behaviors, instead of the other way around. There are also survivors who finally crawl to the healing path on their knees of perfection. Their achievements are outstanding from spending their lives trying to make themselves good enough. They hope the monument of success can bury their pain. Society discredits them and disregards the impact of the experience of abuse too. Success is interpreted as strength gained from the experience of abuse. Success is used against the survivor as much as failure. The bottom line is that society is not going to make room for our pain no matter how we live in it. But we are part of society too, 60 million strong. We can create safe space and live openly so that we can affirm one another and heal together.

February 2

Having a good job, success and friends do not mean that a person is healing. Having great sex does not mean you have dealt with your abuse issues. Forgiving the violator does not mean you have worked through the pain. Being beautiful on the outside does not mean that your wounds are healed. These ways of interacting in the world can distract us from healing because they can distance us from our pain. The external normality helps us avoid what dysfunction is going on inside of us. People who use the façade of normalcy as a distraction may be sensitive to criticism and get easily defensive. They may also attach too easily to others who are in pain and try to save them. They are also likely to be in unhealthy relationships with an attempt to control or be overprotective of their children. These dysfunctional patterns are likely to emerge when a survivor hides rather than heal. It is so much more important that we commit to healing rather than substituting the hard work of healing with external markers to avoid our pain.

February 3

Trust comes easier when it is earned, but survivors often struggle in this area, even learning to trust life, the Universe or God. As survivors, we feel like life itself has let us down. If there is any systematic justice in the world, it sure did not fall upon us. "If such a horrible experience could happen to me as a child, then what force is going to protect me as an adult?" This thought is difficult to grapple with as an adult survivor. The truth is, there is evidence of protection all around us, but we often miss it because we are too focused on the pain. Sometimes survivors attach to the pain as a way to self-protect, believing that holding on to the pain will prevent abuse from happening again. Of course, there is no truth in that belief. Focusing on our pain is likely to paralyze rather than protect. However, we can allow the pain and be present with it, and live with gratitude and awareness of all the good at the same time. When we live with a sense of gratitude, trust is easier.

February 4

There are three common missteps that some survivors take when they get on the healing path. Some survivors sweep people into their lives that have just as much pain as them. They set up a plan to heal together in their mind. But the other person never agrees to this and has no idea that this is even an expectation for the relationship. The targeted person has no intention of traveling a healing path by themselves or with the survivor. They are happy living their life just the way it is. If this is you, you may feel like you are the only one working on your stuff in the relationship. That is true, you are. Your call to healing is a personal one. You cannot force anyone to heal with you. You have to decide if a person is healthy enough to be in a relationship with or not, instead of waiting around for them to heal with you. Other survivors try to force themselves into the lives of others that they know are much further along on the healing path with the hope that they will heal faster. If this is you, you may end up frustrated because the other person may not express the feelings or direct attention toward you that you still need to feel validated. You may also get down on yourself by comparing your healing progress to the other person and deepen a sense of worthlessness. Some survivors stay away from everyone. Unfortunately, this can create a sense of isolation that does not feel good and makes it more challenging to heal. If this is you, you may feel bitter and push people away, then feel resentful that you are alone. All this just means that it is helpful to pay attention to your relationships and your expectations. When you notice patterns that are not working for you, you can be responsible for changing them.

February 5

Some survivors remain in silence because of the negative feelings we have toward the abuser. Many survivors would rather not speak than to admit that they carry a feeling of hate toward the abuser or cannot wait to see the violator dead. Unfortunately, when survivors express anger, it is often rejected as much as expressing pain. There is the false perception that people who are less angry are more healed. In truth, people who are less angry may be in more denial. All feelings can have healthy expressions and denying feelings is not an expression of health. There can be power and resilience in hate and anger. It is often the first feeling that greets us when we come out of denial. Healing does not happen in the absence of anger; it happens in the acceptance of it.

February 6

Healing requires a strong support system because it can get ugly. Survivors often feel worse before they feel better. It is best to have a support system that is not threatened by your healing, without relying on people who have any relationship to the people involved in your abuse. If a family member violated you it is important to develop a support system outside of your family. Often, family members are benefactors of our silence and, therefore, offer resistance to our healing. Too often we delay the healing process according to the signals of support offered to us by people who want to protect rather than heal. We are not all born into a good support system, so we have to consciously create one.

February 7

There are more venues and resources identified for survivors than ever before. However, not every resource is helpful. There are some resources that can be dangerous for survivors. Some survivor services are inconsistent, inaccurate, misleading, or, worst of all, predatory. Survivors must think critically about what it means to have safe space. Every survivor has to find her/his own path. We may reach out in desperation for anything that we can grab a hold of, because anything feels better than the empty space we have lived in for so long. Unfortunately, creating space for survivors to vent about abuse is not the same as safe space. There are many venues, be they books, websites, social network pages, blogs, or in-person support groups that are adult gatherings, online or face-to-face, to share "war wounds." If that is where you are in your healing, then that is fine. In a certain phase of healing, that is what some survivors need. However, to thrive, you need more. You need a lot of information, inspiration, encouragement and adequate support. Try to have an idea of what you are looking for before you join someone offering support. Assess whether they can provide analysis of the experience of childhood sexual abuse as well as language tools to help you find your voice and affirmation for you to use it. Make sure that the support you choose can move you forward, not just support where you are. The person in charge should be a role-model. Every resource that says "For Survivors" will not help you survive, much less thrive. Fortunately, you do get to choose.

February 8

Childhood sexual abuse is a land without consent. Victims, are stripped of self-empowerment. We are transformed into an unsolved Rubik's cube, a three-dimensional mechanical puzzle. The algorithm to restore harmony is too complex, so we adjust to living within the disorderly context. The disorderly context has misconceptions about who we are and what the world offers. Healing helps us take the Rubik Cube challenge. We pay attention to the turns and keep focused on the patterns in our lives. As challenging as the puzzle is, it has been solved by a significant number of people, and many others have come close to solving it. A significant number of survivors are thriving because we have committed to working on the cube. We will restore the harmony in our lives.

FEBRUARY 9

Survivors often come from environments where we are taught and trained to relinquish our personal power in many ways and forms. We often struggle even with the idea of personal power. It is a challenging thought for many survivors. It is easy to do what we have learned, which is to allow someone else to direct our lives. Today is as good a day as any to start paying attention to personal power and claiming it. Think before you say yes or no. Think before you react from a sense of powerlessness. Create a new scenario in your life. Believe in yourself, even when you are not successful the first time. You were born powerful. It is time to recharge.

FEBRUARY 10

The healing path for survivors may include forgiveness. However, forgiveness of the perpetrators is not the right place to start. There is forgiveness of life itself, that life would grant you such pain. When we forgive life, we return to living from a place of gratitude. That will relieve the bitterness. There is forgiveness of self for not knowing how to make the abuse stop. When we place the blame on the violator where it belongs, then we no longer carry the shame. There is forgiveness of those who did not notice our pain just because we did not speak about it. When we begin to process the entire experience of abuse and understand how the environment affected us, we can also come to a place of acceptance that may relieve the anger. Do not feel like you have to take some giant step into forgiveness. Forgiveness does not even work when you force it. You often end up just slipping back into denial. Let forgiveness happen over time and in no particular order of importance when it comes to dealing with the effects of sexual abuse. Forgiveness is not a goal. It arises little by little as enough healing has taken place.

FEBRUARY 11

Childhood sexual abuse and incest begin and end with psychological assault. A trusted adult either made you suffer so much until you offered no defense, or manipulated you through grooming to feel so special that you offered no defense. Either way, the psychological effect is that you end up feeling responsible for their behavior. Since you could not defend yourself, you could not tell. What was left was the psychological assault of guilt and shame that you carried way into adulthood. But it is time to heal.

FEBRUARY 12

The practice of "being present" can be difficult to grasp because it sounds so simple to the mind. "What else can I be but present?" Or, "how can being present bring me peace when there is so much pain in my past that effect my present condition?" These are the types of questions that keep our focus on the pain of the past. Instead, we can try to connect the pain of the past in a meaningful way to the present. When the pain arises, we can bring it into the present instead of focusing on past events with a fixed mindset. Here is one example. When you have a reaction that causes anxiety, fear, anger or some other negative emotion, as soon as you recognize the energy as negative (anything that disturbs your peace even momentarily) just ask yourself a question about your present response. Here are several questions you can ask. You only need to ask one, and the response is not even all that important. They are intended to only raise your awareness. What was I trying to avoid by responding that way? What aspect of myself was I trying to protect? Did that situation remind me of any feelings from my past? Did I confuse this person with a person from my past? Can this moment teach me about who I am now? What can I do to resume my equilibrium that does not require expectations of the person who triggered my response? Remember that the goal is not to solve a problem. The goal is only to be present in the feeling and let the "problem" heal itself over time.

February 13

Healing is not a linear process. Some days our knowledge about psychology and God and loving and being loved is not enough knowing to remove the guilt and shame, fear and anger, or the sense of helplessness and despair. Some days our faith waivers and our strength is depleted. The more we heal, the fewer days we will have like this. So just take a deep breath and know that you are a survivor, even on the worst day.

February 14

The healing path is a special place where participants arrive by invitation only. It is a single invitation. You cannot bring a guest. The invitation goes out to those whose lives are no longer functional in a way that they can pretend to be happy. The sadness, fear, discontent, anger or self-hate has boiled over like an unwatched pot. No one you know in your life is likely to follow you to the path. You will have to learn to love them in their continued dysfunction or let them go. The further you travel on the healing path, the more distance you are likely to create between yourself and those you knew before the path. You have to choose to continue the travel or stay in a spot where you can remain accessible to your loved ones. You cannot hand them your invitation. Only life serves out the invitations.

February 15

We enter the path when we are tired of our pain. We are looking for relief and comfort, but, disappointedly, do not find it on the healing path right away. Many turn away from the healing path once they realize that the pain of healing can be worse than the pain of denial, but only for a while. The payoff of healing is so much greater than the pain of denial. Healing serves you, while denial serves others. The growing pangs of healing will not last forever, but the harm of denial does. So let the healing begin.

February 16

A critical component to stopping childhood sexual abuse is creating a voice and safe space for adult survivors. As long as adult survivors do not feel safe enough to acknowledge the experience of childhood abuse it is senseless to expect a young child to be brave enough to report current abuse. It is no wonder that 70% of cases of child sexual abuse go unreported. Young children lack the vocabulary and authority to speak. In fact, many adult survivors still feel like they lack them as well. That is why 50% of adult survivors never discloses. As a result, information about survivors is absent, and survivors remain fundamentally misunderstood. To the degree that no safe space is created for adult survivors to live openly, perpetrators will continue to rely on victim silence as a primary weapon of abuse. As long as adults are silent, we can expect that children will be silent as well. The choice to live openly does more than help you heal. It helps us heal the world.

February 17

To the degree that we commit to healing, we commit to change. To the degree that we avoid change, we avoid healing. You have to trust the process and let go, revise or edit as you "proofread" your life. Question your relationships and responses to people and the world. Holding on to the familiar patterns because you are afraid of someone's reaction, means that you have granted your personal power to someone else. That is convenient, but not progressive. Who is the director of your life? Who are you still expecting to fulfill you? If the answer is not "you" then the challenges you face will be harder. You will continue to wait to be happy, wait to be rescued, and wait to be free. But you do not have to wait if you work. You have to be patient, but you do not have to wait. You are the master of your fate.

February 18

Not every survivor of childhood sexual abuse has post-traumatic stress, but there are some survivors who have it and do not recognize the symptoms. Just because you do not wake up in the middle of the night screaming, jump every time someone touches you, and do not feel deeply depressed, does not mean you are free of symptoms. Traumatic stress affects the mind and body. There are stress related illnesses, including heart disease, asthma, anxiety, headaches, diabetes and gastrointestinal problems. Survivors have higher incidences of these illnesses than the rest of the population. Social isolation or awkwardness and anxiety are also related to PTSD.

February 19

Living life bigger than your past means more than just not thinking about the past. Most of the effect of the abuse occur on a psychological level that is beyond our consciousness. Survivors do not "consciously" relive the abuse to respond to life situations. Memories become attached to our bodies as well as our brains and create automatic responses. These responses do not require "thinking," any more than a dog "thinks" about standing by to the door when it wants to go out to poop. Reliving the abuse is a response, even if it is not rational in our minds. This response thinking can be re-trained by healing. Healing is the practice of acceptance, coming to terms with the thoughts and the pain that comes with them. Then we transmute it all into beauty within ourselves that everyone slowly starts to notice.

February 20

At times, the pain of healing may feel greater than living in silence, and you may wonder if it is worth it. You may have felt more accepted when you were silence. You may have ignored the nagging sense of shame when you were living in denial. You may have felt "happier" when no one knew of your struggle to "fit in." Now that you are trying to live in truth, your world may feel like it is falling apart. It is not. It is just reorganizing. No mechanic can repair your car without taking out parts. The mechanic may have to take out three parts just to get to the part that needs to be repaired. In that case, it may take a while, and you may need to find alternative modes of moving about in the world. It is inconvenient, but well worth it to have a reliable car. So it is with healing. You cannot see the mechanic, so you have to trust the process of healing. Life itself is the mechanic. However, you are an active participant in the repair. Allow life to rearrange itself as you get to the parts that need the most repairing.

FEBRUARY 21

The next time you feel like the child who experienced the abuse (afraid, needy, angry) instead of like your adult self, just imagine her/ him in your mind and say "Thank you for getting me this far" before you let the grown up take over. Give the child her/his props. She/he is not the one blocking you from healing. Instead, it may be your rejection of her/him may be keeping you stuck or causing friction on the healing path. Make room in your life for you wounded child to heal. The adult self cannot heal without that. When you heal the inner child, you are more likely to thrive.

FEBRUARY 22

People who experience trauma from community catastrophes tend to heal faster than people who experience trauma alone. For example, people who were directly impacted by 911 or Hurricane Katrina are more likely to heal than an individual that has a child who dies. The difference in healing is the perception of "responsibility." When trauma is collective, it is easier for people to see the big picture and not take personal responsibility for it. Victims also collaborate to heal, often with public recognition. The world pulls for them and prays for them as their pain is affirmed. People who suffer from individual trauma often experience the opposite. A parent whose child dies is likely to feel guilty for not personally doing enough to prevent the death, even if all the evidence is to the contrary. Society is also more likely to speculate about the cause of the trauma instead of assuming the complete innocence of the parent. Survivors of childhood sexual abuse are likewise subjected to personal rather than a collective perspective of trauma. However, the trauma of the abuse is collective, even though it is experienced as an individual. Violators collect victims one at a time, but there are 60 million survivors of this collective trauma. What was done to you has been done to others within this system of sexual violence. However cruel the violator may have been, there are many violators equally cruel in this system of sexual violence around the world. There are many families that condone it, cultures that promote it, and communities that ignore it. There are collective denial and ignorance that often supports the collective victimization. The good news is that we can also heal collectively.

February 23

If you know that you are in pain, then you are the "knowing," you are not the pain. Many people live miserable lives and do not even know it? They have become the pain. There is no recognition that life should be different? They keep trying to manipulate others instead of reach for higher ground themselves. We are the "strive" in striving to be better. We are the "heal" in healing. We are the "sent" in present. We are present to heal. You know that pain is part of the process. So allow yourself to be in the process.

February 24

We try so hard to heal. Maybe we try too hard sometimes. As we learn to heal without judgment, we will not count our failures. We will monitor our risk-taking. As we learn to offer no resistance to the challenges we face we will not see the world in terms of good experiences and bad experiences. We will play with the universe as a co-creator. We can stop trying to heal and just be present with what life brings. We can stop trying to make relationships work and just be present in them. We can stop trying so hard to be right and just allow ourselves to be present. We can be fully in love with ourselves as we pay close attention.

FEBRUARY 25

Some days you just feel defeated, like this stuff is never going to get any better. Some days you just feel so much pain, confusion, and frustration that you cannot see or feel good. The good news is that even those days, you are still healing. Those are simply days that you are stuck in the traffic jam of healing. But you are still on the journey. Healing does not make every day perfect. Healing teaches us to greet each day without resistance and pay attention to the information the day brings so that we can apply it to our lives.

FEBRUARY 26

There is a double jeopardy that comes with living openly. People often prefer our silence. They directly or indirectly request us to move through relationships as if our childhood history does not matter. We try our best to compartmentalize our healing. However, every time we bring up legitimate complaints about the relationship or people's behavior, they remember that we have a history of childhood sexual abuse. They use our history of sexual abuse as an excuse not to address issues that we raise. Critics readily connect our history of abuse to any problems they have with us. Yet, we are often dismissed when we connect our experience of sexual abuse to current problems. We are often used as a scapegoat. Another burden falls upon the survivor, which is to educate those within our environment to respond appropriately to us as survivors. If people within our environments cannot provide safe space, they should avoid discriminating by dismissing us based on our experience of abuse.

February 27

Being a survivor of childhood sexual abuse does not make people stronger. There are fantastic people in the world who have not had the suffering that survivors have had. This level of suffering is not required. Moreover, there are too many survivors who never even make it to the healing path. The experience takes them to a dark place, and they remain there the rest of their lives. Today, we are stronger because we are on the healing path. On the healing path, we are likely to make more meaning of life and find a purpose. That comes as a result of being a survivor, not a victim.

February 28

Commitment and alertness are requirements for healing. You must commit to healing each day. Some days you heal a tiny weenie bit, and other days you heal a lot of bits. But you commit the same each day. When you commit to healing, you commit to seeking the truth about yourself, life and people. Seeking truth feels much different from seeking power and control or seeking safety and comfort. Truth seeking is vulnerability and openness. That is why you must stay alert. You must use alertness to see what you do not want to see and feel what you are trying not to feel. Without commitment and alertness, you are likely to default back to your old defense patterns for self-protection.

February 29

Often we pick up language because we hear it so much. We do not give language much thought most of the time. However, the language we use to describe our experiences does matter. Our brain processes words, often in their most simplistic form. So what we say may matter more than we think. For survivors, referring to a violator as "my" violator continues a bind with the person in our mind. Violators do not belong to us. They are not ours. They usually have dozens or even hundreds of victims, not just us. So one tiny change we can make in our healing journey is to change the language when we refer to people who violated us. "The person who violated me" rather than "my violator" can have an impact on the mind. In healing we need all the help we can get. So why not include the language.

3: IN YOUR SKIN

There is no evidence that sexual preference is caused by sexual abuse. If the victims were gay or lesbian before victimization, they would remain that way afterward. If the victims were heterosexual before victimization, they would remain so afterward.

March 1

I can accept that I am a powerless individual, so powerless that I could not protect myself. Or, I was not completely powerless, and I could have prevented what happened. The dichotomy often becomes a big struggle of belief at some point in our healing. This is often the big "IT" in the "I cannot accept it" statement that survivors often make. No one wants to feel so vulnerable that they can be manipulated into betraying their sense of right and wrong. On the other hand, one wants to be responsible for their abuse. Survivors do not want to accept either of these conditions. Neither condition makes you feel safe in the world. But the truth is that violators are more manipulative than children are powerful. You are no longer a powerless child. Now you are a powerful healing adult making your own decisions. But you only have the power to heal what has been done, not to prevent it. No matter how powerful you become, the abuse will never be your fault.

March 2

Healing is not just a matter of the heart. The brain is involved in our trauma. Every experience we have makes a connection to our brain, whether or not we can remember the experience. We respond to the connections with feelings, expectations, and behaviors. So creating positive healing experiences with information, exercise, nutrition, hope and affirmations will stimulate the brain and create a shift. This shift does not happen overnight. But it can happen.

March 3

As we heal, we put together pieces of the puzzle of our dysfunctional and distorted childhood. The pieces take us years to gather and fit into our understanding of our current lives. When we disclose, we disclose as if we knew all of the facts that we have taken years to discover. So people cannot understand all that we did not know because we tell them what we now know. Many of our situations are so complex that it would take hours of speaking to even begin to unravel our experience for the listener. No one will listen for that long. The details that we discover are more important to us than to anyone else. As we uncover details, we must shower ourselves with compassion and understanding so that it does not matter who else understands.

March 4

One of the biggest challenges of healing is going within to find your resolve, your peace, your comfort. Looking for the external world to give us affirmation is a setup. At times, we do not draw support from people because we cannot convince ourselves that we deserve to be heard, that we are not guilty and should not feel ashamed. We cannot expect people to understand and believe what we have not yet accepted. Sometimes people simply reflect back to us what we already believe. Once you accept the truth of your innocence and your significance and your right to heal, you will find people who support you, or who reflect your truth back to you.

March 5

Most of us learn how to live beyond the pain. Thank goodness, we do not take our life even though we may fantasize about suicide. We push our bodies out of bed every morning and make the best of our day while our dark minds filled with self-doubt and fear await our return when our head reunite with our pillow. We build careers, raise children, and maintain friendships as we live beyond our pain. However, peace only comes when we transmute our pain. You cannot transmute pain by ignoring it. The opposite is true. You must hold it present and analyze its content. Only then can you turn it into a goldmine of peace.

March 6

"Why did this happen to me?" Do you ask this question from a place of resistance or a place of acceptance? When this question comes from a place of resistance survivors get stuck in a state of disbelief and may experience emotional paralysis. They may be waiting for someone to come along and save them. Contrarily, when we ask this question from a place of acceptance we open ourselves up to allow truth in so that we can move forward. We may look at why it happened in a concrete way. We may evaluate the environment in which the abuse took place. We may explore the roles that people played in covering up or ignoring what was happening. We may try to understand how the secret was kept. The goal is to understand oneself within the healing process. When we ask the question from this place of acceptance, we allow more questions to arise in a state of readiness for whatever it triggers in us. We trust the process to heal.

March 7

Most people who move from surviving to thriving elicit a lot of help. Help can come in many shapes and sizes. But the survivor has to move toward help. Rarely will help come knocking at your door. Help often comes in the way of reading books, including books on tape. Some of the best healing books do not mention sexual abuse. Healing is healing. Living harmoniously and authentically and living in the present are the common components of healing no matter what the past has brought you. It is fine to turn your focus away from sexual abuse specifically to learn how to live generally in peace. That does not mean that you ignore the sexual abuse at all. It means that the sexual abuse becomes embedded within the context of what it means to live in peace. You can explore the sexual abuse from a context of healing rather than explore healing from a context of sexual abuse. Either way may work for you. But if you find yourself stuck on one path, take a detour.

March 8

Emotions are neither good nor bad. They provide us with information or call us to pay attention. When we allow ourselves to be present with the emotion, then it can lead us to our intuition. We use the emotion to explore within rather than react. We know when we are lead to intuition because when we resolve the issue, the emotion fades away. However, many times emotions lead to the use of ego defense instead, so even if there is resolve, you remain emotionally charged. If you find yourself emotionally charged even after resolution, then your emotions are using you.

March 9

When we live with acceptance of abuse, it may (or may not) look like this. We feel no shame about our experience, nor pride. Being a survivor of sexual abuse is an experience. We do not need to wear it as a badge of honor since none of us would ever volunteer for such a plight. We do not need to hide it either because we were not active participants. We were victims. Now we are survivors who accept the experience because to resist it would be fighting the wind.

March 10

Most survivors of childhood sexual abuse are incest survivors, but we hate to use the word because of the stereotypes associated with it. Incest is never voluntary when it involves a person under the age of eighteen. When we avoid using the word, we inadvertently contribute to the myth of stranger danger. Avoiding the word (incest) may also keep us in denial of our experience by dismissing the trauma.

March 11

Violators often live above scrutiny while survivors live in silence. On the outside violators may appear gentle, while survivors appear weak. Violators often appear cooperative, while survivors appear rebellious. Violators appear vibrant while survivors appear depressed. Violators may appear productive while victims appear apathetic. Violators walk the earth feeling free and protected while survivors walk the earth with fear and insecurity. Violators get more support in the world than survivors. They are better protected in the world. It is time to change this reality. There is a paradigm shift on the horizon where survivors will take back their power. We will change what it means to be a survivor. Survivors will live in silence no more. We will show our strength and solidarity and lift our voice to say We Are Not Victims Anymore!

MARCH 12

There is not much room for fear, mistrust and doubt on the healing path if you want to thrive. When you recognize your ability to take care of yourself and create safe space for yourself, you do not rely so heavily on trusting others to take care of you. You will take care of you, no matter what the situation entails. You do not give away your power by depending on other people to live up to your expectations to be happy. You do not fear much because you trust yourself. Do not worry if you are not in this space yet. You have not yet reached this far on the journey. Keep traveling and you will.

MARCH 13

The mind is our most useful tool for healing. The mind is also our biggest obstacle. The less we use our mind, the more effective our healing will be. When we use our mind for productive thinking, we heal. However, most of the thoughts that pass through our mind do not serve us well. They do not protect us from harm, connect us to people, or move us forward. Often our brain is on hyper-alert and does a lot of chattering about the world that causes us anxiety. Mind chatter interferes with thinking. Chatter consists of endless warnings, objections, and assumptions about other people. Chatter does not move us forward in healing. Learning to decrease the chatter can move us forward. See if you can notice the difference between mind chatter and thinking. Practice requires you to remain present and in-tuned to your mind. Meditation is a great practice for this.

March 14

The system of sexual abuse is quite complex. Secrecy, betrayal, male-dominance, neglect and misuse of authority all contribute to the uniquely common experience of childhood sexual abuse. So healing has to address all of the issues at some point. Healing also has to address relationships between all of the people involved, not just the physical touch by the perpetrator. This system is so complex that it usually takes many years for us to explore our experiences. Much of healing is about finding and turning over the pieces to the puzzle of childhood so that we can understand the present. So, trying to explain our personal experience to others in a way that they can understand what we have not yet discovered is a challenge. Your time is better spent in self-discovery and understanding than trying to get others to understand. Those that want to support us will do so in the absence of understanding.

March 15

Human trafficking happens all over the world and includes prostitution at a local level. It is called trafficking because a violator sometimes removes the victim from their hometown and forces them into prostitution. The victims are not usually taken out of the country or state. They are taken just far enough away where they cannot travel back home. Many victims barely reach their teenage years before being captured. There are many victims of trafficking that do not become survivors. Sometimes they die under the thumb of a pimp, sometimes from drug addiction. Sometimes victims even go to prison. Some end up in long-term abusive relationships. Sometimes they just sleepwalk the rest of their lives. These are our forgotten brothers and sisters that often do not make it to the healing path. They receive even less support than other survivors, no matter what age they were trafficked. The stereotypes that we hold about prostitutes prevent connections that link us all back to the prevalence of childhood sexual abuse. It also makes survivors of human trafficking less likely to identify as survivors of childhood sexual abuse because we live with the myth that prostitution is voluntary. However, no sexual contact between an adult and a child is voluntary or reasonable. Survivors of human trafficking are in as much need of the healing path as any of us. We must encourage survivors to heal together and lift up one another no matter what brings us to the path.

March 16

If only being a survivor were our only challenge in life, but it is not. Being a survivor is the challenge in life that makes all other challenges more difficult to face. Breakups trigger a fear of abandonment. Job loss taps our sense of powerlessness. Parenting issues raise questions about our genetic worthiness. Major life issues make being a survivor feel worse. The good news is that as we heal from the trauma of childhood sexual abuse, we start to face all challenges with powerful outlooks that move us forward. Once we refuse to be a victim, then nothing victimizes us.

March 17

There is a point in time that you knew you were participating in a deviant relationship with the violator. You think you agreed, acquiesced, and complied. You may even believe that you initiated the relationship. Self-blame is the feedback your adult mind feeds you. But this remembrance is the voice of the violator that groomed you. Guilt is the result of the grooming by the perpetrator. You have to go back further in your mind to see the truth of victimization. You have to go back to the mind of your inner child. You have to remember the questions that the violator asked, the generosity imposed, the threats, the lies, and all the other manipulation that created the "relationship." There was no more a relationship that you contributed to than the elderly woman whose purse is snatched by the mugger who helps her with her grocery bags.

March 18

The cards have been stacked against us for healing. Our screams have never been heard and our silence is deafening. We behave as if everything is OK so that the world can pretend that everything is OK. But, the world has not been OK for a long time. Female genital mutilation is the oldest practice to deny the sexual pleasure of females. Then there was the practice of fathers deciding who the daughters would marry, thus have sex with, whether they wanted to or not. The sex slave trade is one of the oldest and most profitable businesses around the world, with most victims being put to work as children (males and females). These accepted practices that have lingered on in the world are indeed connected to what goes on in households, in churches, and on dates. We are not just talking about healing ourselves to stop our own pain. Our pain is connected to the pain from thousands of years ago. Our voice can prevent pain for thousands of years to come. Our voice is bigger than our personal experience. It is the collective story about the absence of bodily autonomy that we must begin to tell. We must shed light on the history that led us here.

March 19

Survivors who try to follow the media model of relationships may find themselves in frustrated because their survival defenses may not allow them to play certain roles of masculinity or femininity. On the other hand, if survivors have a caring enough partner, then the relationship could become a practice of healing. Ultimately, the only way anyone knows that they are truly ready for a relationship is to be in one. You can heal for years alone, but not reach a point where you are ready to partner with another person. This does not mean that you should run out and find a relationship. But it may mean that you do not have to spend the next five years trying to fix your life before you allow yourself to be in a relationship.

March 20

There are cycles of life, and sometimes the cycles feel more like circles. You may feel like you have made no progress because the same situations upset you or you notice the same dysfunctional patterns of behavior in yourself, or your feelings return to anger or shame after you thought you had resolved them. It is in these times that you must trust the process. If you know that you have been actively involved in the healing process, then it is impossible for you to end up in the same space you once were. Awareness and intention move us, slowly but surely. You may be experiencing similarity in your cycle, but progress has been made, and healing is going on, still.

March 21

Healing moves us from child victim behaviors toward responsible adult behaviors. Many of the behaviors that we adopted as children to help us survive are no longer useful. We have to pay close attention to the behaviors that we adopted as children that cause us pain today. We did not have healthy choices as children because other people were guiding our lives. However, as adults, we are supposed to guide our lives. When we give that responsibility to another person, then we are embracing the victim behaviors that we adopted long ago. Only we can change our patterns. We cannot wait for the world to be kind, understanding, or rescue us. We change from being a victim to being a survivor by the choices that we make each day. Each decision that we make benefits our growth or our victimization. If our life is still full of pain and despair, we are likely making decisions that benefit our victimization, which includes the 'nondecisions' that we make, like not speaking up. The world is a cruel place for anyone who does not self-protect with the choices that they make. If you allow just anybody in your space without boundaries, then bad people will use up that space. If you choose to follow people who bring you harm, they will use you up and suck you dry. Peace and prosperity only come through the decisions that you make as an adult. As long as those decisions mimic the decisions we made when we were helpless children, then we will remain helpless adults. Make decisions that leave you feeling empowered, not disempowered. Change the decisions that you make and you will change your healing path.

March 22

Many survivors grow up feeling like we are not normal. We attach our healing to the possibility that we will feel normal if people believe or understand us. We seek validation of our experience. Unfortunately, we mostly do not get what we seek. Our healing has to be internal, with internal validation. We owe no sort of explanation to the perpetrators or the people who support them, for breaking our silence. We do not need to make space or opportunity for the perpetrator to understand how their behavior affected us, at least not as a requirement to heal. If we are going to seek compassion and understanding, we should seek it where it is "normal" to give it freely, places like "Talking Trees, Inc." We should not seek healthy support from unhealthy people. Go where there is no convincing to be done. Do not try to force your healing into your expectations of others who have been invested in your silence, such as perpetrators.

March 23

The reason we disclose is to live in our truth. We cannot predict or control how anyone will respond to disclosure of the truth. Maybe the person will use the information to better understand us, or maybe they will use the information to blame us or shame us. We do not know. So if we disclose with a specific purpose in mind other than living in our truth, we risk setting ourselves up for disappointment. There is freedom that comes with truth when you create space for truth in your life. However, truth sometimes requires a lot of alone space when others are not ready to live in the space with you. So you must be ready to live alone in your truth rather than living in a circle of lies with others. Those of us who live openly have made our choice.

March 24

Healing does not require a fight of any sort. In fact, healing requires the opposite. Healing calls for survivors to offer no resistance. Offer no resistance to acknowledging your needs. You have the right to tell someone "no." Offer no resistance to your uncomfortable feelings. You have the right to speak your mind. Offer no resistance to identifying as a survivor. You have the right to find your voice. Offer no resistance to your pain. You have the right to cry.

March 25

How small have you made yourself to fit into "their space?"

Every time you deny your right to feel, you deny your right to heal. Every time you refuse to speak to protect the secret, you weaken your sense of self. Every time you share space with the violator in denial to be part of a larger group (family, organization, etc.) you compromise your integrity. You feel the nudges at your heart and in your mind. It is not the abuse that is making you miserable because that is indeed in the past. However, each time to make a present decision to protect secrets of your past you dig a deeper hole of denial that keeps you tied to the past. The after effect of the choices that you now make as a result of the abuse can keep you in trauma for life. We cannot change the past, but we must become conscious of the decisions we make in the present to direct our future.

March 26

Do not make being a survivor into an identity. Surviving sexual abuse is a horrible experience. We did not choose it, nor did we earn it. Survivor is not a badge of honor. We were victims. If we turn that into an identity, then we are more likely to hold onto a victim mentality. What we did when we were victims helped us to survive. But those patterns of behavior are not necessarily going to help us thrive. So we do not want to hold onto a survivor identity either. We can use an identity to heal, but we should not attach to an identity to live. We can heal our way into thriving mode, but only if we do not attach ourselves to survivor identity.

March 27

Breaking the silence is a personal experience that each individual has to figure out (not all in one day). Learning how to break the silence is a challenge, but the first step is intent. You should have the intention to break the commitment you made to secrecy and silence in your heart, then let your mind figure out how to do it. Some survivors confront their violators. Other survivors start a website. There are survivors who let their art speak for them. Some survivors start their disclosure with a therapist while others start with their partners. Breaking silence is also a process that is continual. There are ongoing decisions to make, like how much detail you want to share, and how to avoid responding to questions about personal details you are not ready to disclose. Wherever you are in breaking the silence, appreciate that space.

March 28

Healing is a lifetime commitment. In a world that values speed above quality, it is easy to want to be "fixed" right now. We want the fastest technology and it is never fast enough. We feed our children fast food, so they do not have to wait to eat. We love the microwave. We expect an immediate response to "instant messaging." We have sex on the first date. We shop online to avoid waiting in line. All of this hurrying just leads to more hurrying, and often more pain. Slow down and allow healing to happen. Pay attention and you will notice your growth. Stop listening for the "done" button. Healing is a process. Trust it, embrace it and live in it.

March 29

Fear can save your life, or fear can ruin it. Fear is intended to caution us, not paralyze us. We are not supposed to live in fear for long periods of time, certainly not our entire lives. The fear response is to give us the strength to fight hard or run away. When fear freezes us, we are likely to not survive. The fear response is also intended to alarm us of life threats. Most of what we fear today is not life-threatening. We are often afraid of making mistakes, being alone and afraid of failure. These are all parts of life. We do not want to fear life. If our fear paralyzes us, then we are no longer living. Just because we are still breathing does not mean we are living. We become the walking dead, and fear is no longer protecting us. It is time to return to the land of the living.

March 30

Some children may be easier targets for multiple victimizations, but it is not because they are the cause of abuse. It is because perpetrators rely on environmental cues to violate a child as much as much as a child's vulnerability. Children who have been abused once are likely to be in an environment where abuse is ignored. Meanwhile, the child has to sort out a lot of unexpected and confusing patterns about other people's behavior as well as their response to the behaviors. There is too much information for their minds to consider. For example, children who have a tendency to shut down emotionally and have fewer friends are more likely to be taken advantage of by sexual predators. Abuse usually happens within dysfunctional families where children are often left unprotected for long or regular periods of time. Violators target unprotected children. There is no limit to the number of violators who will take advantage of any particular child either. Over 50% of survivors have more than one violator. The average number of violators before the age of 18 is three. Victims do not invite the abuse. Perpetrators know and practice their deviance with as many as 100 victims that they carefully choose to manipulate. Children's minds cannot compete with the mind of adults who set out to harm.

March 31

You do not get rid of emotional pain as you do a headache. There is no magic pill to take and no immediate relief. We have to transmute emotional pain into positive energy, which takes a lot of time. We can transmute it into compassion for oppressed people everywhere. We can transmute our pain into advocacy work and make the world a safer place. Pain can also make a graceful dancer or prolific writer. Pain can even be transmuted into the discipline necessary to become a medical doctor. Pain does not always paralyze; it can also transform.

4: FAMILY AFFAIRS

Survivors choose many variations of "no contact" to meet their healing needs. Some survivors have no physical contact, but may allow infrequent contact. Some survivors tell their family that they are going "no contact" and others cut off communication without notice. No contact is a tool that some survivors utilize as they unravel the tangled web of confusion, manipulations, and co-dependence that they have learned to cope.

April 1

"Can I have time to think?" This is a legitimate response to any request, new information or uncomfortable situation. Since many of us live with a hyper-response brain system, we often treat every situation as if it is urgent. But what we do in an urgent situation is different from a day to day response, at least, it should be. Typically, situations that are urgent need to be controlled or contained, whereas, day-to-day situations need compromise and consistency. When we say yes we need to know that we can follow through on what is being asked of us, not just responding to a fear that the person may not like us if we say no. So making a habit of giving yourself time to think can change relationships, at home, at work, and with yourself.

April 2

We have no obligation to protect violators or the people who love them. We have a responsibility to heal. Healing is not about revenge or destroying anyone. Healing is about making the world a better place even if it means making our inner circle less secure. People who feel exposed through us healing have to face the same opportunity as we did. They get to choose to live in truth or keep finding ways to protect their lie. But, we are not obligated to remain a part of anyone's lies. Living openly does not destroy lives. Violating children and silencing adults destroy lives.

April 3

There are memories held in your subconscious for you because they are too painful to your conscious mind. This forgotten load is called repressed memories. There are many ways that repressed memories can play out for adult survivors. Survivors who had more than one perpetrator may only remember the first or last violator. Survivors who remember all of the violators may repress some of the actual events or the duration of the abuse. For example, survivors may remember the abuse starting at age eight instead of four. Some survivors do not remember any events but remember their responses as well as people and places related to the event. Repressed memories take many forms for survivors, which add to the complexity of healing.

April 4

All sexual abuse is horrible. No one can determine how entitled you are to grieve based on your physical experience. It does not matter if there was no penetration or if the contact was not "forced" because you never put up a physical fight. It does not matter that you did not figure out that you were abused until you became an adult. It does not matter if the violator was the same age as you. You are still an adult survivor of childhood sexual abuse. You cannot heal by denying yourself the right to acknowledge your "brokenness."

April 5

The process of healing is a complex system. We need information, practice, and support. Trying to create a life that involves all three is not easy. The information needs to be personally relevant. For example, the healing process for victims who are raped as adults may not necessarily be personally relevant for incest survivors. Practicing new behaviors requires safe space and tolerance for risk. You have to have some sense of certainty that no one is standing over you waiting to take advantage of your mistakes. You have to have enormous support to consistently engage in the healing process. Do not be too hard on yourself when the process slows down. The conditions are rarely stable.

April 6

Abuse of women and children has been a part of (in)humanity since the beginning of time. Women and children largely have been viewed as possessions of men. There are many books about this historical reality. Part of male empowerment historically has centered on sexual prowess in a variety of ways. Many ways have been inhumane including, castration of disempowered men (such as slaves), the raping of women and children, a multi-billion dollar sex trade industry that consists largely of children, and the animalistic practice of engaging in consensual sex with detached emotion from one's partner. The fact that 90% of violators are males, even when the victims are male, speaks to the harmful practices of male dominance. Most men do not actively participate in these practices, but many may contribute to the silence of victims. But it is time to break the silence and let the healing begin.

April 7

When the pain is so deep that you are ready to die, that can be such a pivotal point because death is a natural process. The feeling of wanting to die is not meant to be a physical death. It is meant to be a death of the ego. It is meant to be the death of the imposter mind that developed to protect you but is now yielding dysfunction. The ego has run out of defenses to survive. It is signaling to you that you must take a different path. Now you must learn to live authentically, without your defenses. The point is not to advance your physical demise. The desire for death is about transition, not ending. The point is to let the dead leaves fall off of your tree and prepare for the spring bloom, after the long winter. Let relationships that do not serve you die. Let your assumption that the world will fall apart if you do not keep it together die. Let your longing and searching for what you lost in childhood die (but not your inner child). Let your codependency die. Let your fears die. The ego has lived a long life of dysfunction on your behalf. Now it is confused about the calling for its own death. Your spirit can feel the calling for an awakening.

April 8

Dismiss those who accuse you of using abuse as a crutch to blame all of your faults and undesirable behaviors on. Tell them to read the research. People often overlook our triumph and what it has taken for us to live as mentally stable as we do. The truth is a lot more of our baggage is related to the abuse than we even realize. Abuse is not a crutch; it is an influential experience in our lives. Post-traumatic stress is a reality for many survivors that we keep "hidden." We keep it so well-hidden that when our faults surface people often accuse us of intentionally behaving with patterns of dysfunction. They refuse to believe that we have social anxiety, that viewing sexual aggression on television is a trigger or that seeing little children sitting on an adult's lap make us depressed. Why would anyone want to make this up and choose to randomly adopt patterns of behavior that cause conflict? It is silly to assume that survivors are faking trauma.

April 9

You need someone to understand you. But that someone does not have to be a person who lives in your house. You need someone to talk with you. But conversations do not have to take place in person. You need knowledge about how to thrive. But that knowledge does not have to be written in a book. You need a supportive environment. However, that environment does not have to be permanent. Instead of focusing on the lack, take a good look at your life and write down resources that you can use to heal. Forget about what you think healing should look like if you do not have the resources to make it so. Focus on the resources that you do have. The question then becomes, "How can I use this to heal?" When we start with that question, we travel the healing path differently than when we focus on our obstacles.

April 10

Have you ever been at home at night in a storm and the electricity goes out (I reside Iowa, so that happens a lot)? When that happens, you are placed in darkness for a period. At that moment, all of the comforts in your environment become a temporary danger. You do not want to get out of your bed and bump into the dresser or trip over the expensive rug or bang your elbow on the imported lamp. Well, sexual abuse causes a "power" failure. For some victims, the light never returns; they die in darkness. The truth is we do not all make it to the healing path. But if you are reading this, you are a survivor. Your light has been restored. It is safe to move about the world. Notice that children often remain afraid for the rest of the night and insist on sleeping with parents because they do not trust that the light is going to remain. Like children, survivors have difficulty trusting the light after being subjected to periods of darkness. Healing teaches us to live in the light.

April 11

What would you do if you knew with 100% certainty that the risks you took would yield you the result you wanted or needed to change your life? Well, that is why it is called risk, because there is no certainty. If you do not succeed at first, evaluate and revise accordingly, then stick your neck out again. We, as survivors, have a tendency to overrate the need for safety in a way that prevents us from taking risks. When you have grown up feeling unsafe, taking risks feels foolish or scary. But overemphasized safety can put us at risk of remaining miserable.

April 12

You are the architect of your life. You are the creator and builder. The decisions you make today defines your life more than past experiences. Understanding your past helps you to understand how you got where you are today. But it does not define where you go tomorrow. If you are not interested in reliving your past, then you may have to let go of the people of your past, regardless of their title or role in your life. Sometimes letting go of the people of your past may create enough space in your life to begin to rebuild. You have to acquire some new skills and building materials, such as communication and behavioral patterns, as well as a mindset to customize your life in a way that makes you want to be in it. Every day when you wake up, put on your construction hat before you get out of bed. Get up and build. A beautiful life awaits.

April 13

No one needs childhood trauma to become a strong person. Being a survivor is not what made you a strong person. Being a strong person is what made you a survivor. We do not need to try to find any justice or make any sense of being a survivor. We just are. What we make of our past is not nearly as important as how we live in the present. That does not mean the past is not important. The past is important. It is just not as important as the present. Everyone has a history that contributes to their present. Not everyone with a good past has a good present. Not everyone with a bad past has a bad present. No one has a history that completely determines their present, no matter how good or how bad the past was. Our present decisions have the last say.

April 14

The wonderful truth about the healing path is that it does not require anyone's belief but your own. You are the only one, ultimately, that has to believe that you deserve to heal. Then invite others along for the ride. Those who want to support you will stay. Others may refuse to support you and find their exit out of your life. You will not even have to ask them to leave. Just do not ask them to stay.

April 15

Today is Safe Space Day all around the world. Safe Space Day was created in 2010 in Iowa as a way to recognize and honor the resilience of adult survivors of childhood sexual abuse. We all get to celebrate wherever we are with who we like, and in whatever way feels good to us. However, if you ever have an opportunity to celebrate by attending this national event, then this could be a life-changing experience. Today is a day to remember that healing does not require you to forget about the abuse. Willingness to remember is where healing occurs, instead of trying to forget. Remember that you did not give up. Happy Safe Space Day.

April 16

Your perception that pain is happening as a result of how people currently treat you is only partly correct. People do betray, take for granted, hurt, disappoint, etc. However, all healing and prevention come from within. When we pay attention to what is going on within us, we become less vulnerable to the external factors that would otherwise threaten us. We can start by questioning our motives. What are you looking to gain when you befriend people? What caused you to trust someone despite the evidence that they are untrustworthy? Why did you offer the person space in your life and give them control over your emotions? Who are you trying to please with your decisions? These types of questions relate to your ability to trust yourself, rather than solely rely on people to be trustworthy. You should be able to trust yourself to make comfortable decisions about the emotional space that you offer to people. So you have to pay attention to what is happening internally, not just externally.

April 17

We must tell both sides of the story. Yes, childhood abuse

creates trauma and leaves the surviving adult with particular challenges that are related to brain activity, not just feelings. However, we must be careful about creating a misunderstanding that every survivor of childhood abuse is traumatized permanently. We must be careful that we do not see ourselves as "damaged." We want our pain to be recognized, but not stigmatized. Many, if not most, survivors live as well as people who were not traumatized during childhood. Most people who were abused as children do not become abusers. Being abused as a child is not the only reason people harm, and being a victim does not cause a person to abuse someone in the future (correlation does not equal causation). As we analyze connections through research, it is important that survivors of childhood sexual abuse do not allow themselves to be defined by research results.

April 18

You are strong. That is why you are still here. You did not survive because you were weak, afraid, stupid, or unlovable. Do not accept those labels or interpretations of your healing experience. You have nothing else to prove to anyone, not even to yourself. The task is to use your strength, courage, intellect and lovingness to heal instead of using it all up on others and then feeling empty.

April 19

The wounds of childhood sexual abuse do not end when the violator stops the physical contact. They are not like a broken leg that the doctor puts a cast on for a certain period and then it heals like new. The effects of childhood sexual abuse are more like an autoimmune disease, a life-long illness where the body cannot distinguish between good cells and bad cells. So antigens that are supposed to fight bad cells in the body attack good cells in the body. Attacking good cells can create a flare-up of symptoms. Patients can treat the symptoms that arise and live as healthy as they can at any point in time, but cannot cure the illness. The goal is to live with as few flare-ups as possible by maintaining a healthy lifestyle. Likewise, adult survivors of childhood sexual abuse are life-long healers. Even the healthiest lifestyle does not fully protect us from occasional flare-ups. We should never forget that we are healing, not healed.

April 20

People do matter since human beings are social creatures by nature. Not many people are happy being alone. Still, you are responsible for your happiness. Part of that responsibility is drawing people into your life that can bring out the joy in you, rather than constantly trigger your fears and insecurities. People cannot bring us joy, but they can open space for us to create it. We have to carefully construct our social lives so that we have joy in them.

April 21

There are those days that you wish for medical intervention, divine intervention, a magic pill or hypnosis to stop what is going on in your head. There must be a way to stop this pain without destroying me in the process. Drugs, sex, alcohol, and food are tempting but too temporary. Tears and fears consume you. Just hold on until those moments pass, even if those moments last for days or months or years. They will pass. The magic is in the holding on and offering no resistance to the moment.

April 22

There is an embedded scene in your head that triggers guilt

and shame. You think of it randomly and often. It is the scene where you see yourself with the violator. You see the "self" that brings you the shame and self-hate. This moment of shame you must face. I can assure you that there is information that is hidden in this re-play moment that you cannot see because you keep trying to turn away from it. When you turn away from this moment, it separates your child self from your adult self. This is the moment that the adult and child self must see eye-to-eye on instead of the adult blaming the inner child. This moment when triggered, is seen through an adult interpretation and does not account for the systemic abuse or neglect that was present in the child's life. It does not account for the fear that was induced in the child's heart. It does not account for the confusion that was induced in the child's mind. Are you ready to see the child's trauma and truth? Are you ready to see the child's resilience and survival? The next time you are triggered with guilt and shame by this haunting moment, stop and take a closer look and see what you have been missing.

April 23

One important aspect of healing is facing fear. Fear of being alone, fear of making a mistake, fear of being vulnerable, fear of being insignificant, and fear of conflict, can lead us to cling to people, places and things that do not suit our best interest. Unfortunately, when many people say, "I love you" they mean "I'm afraid of you leaving." When most people say, "I hate you" they often mean "I fear the vulnerability this relationship brings out in me." Sometimes when people say "I'm sorry" they often mean "I fear the conflict this could bring." Some people say "no" when they mean "I'm afraid of making a mistake." We all experience fear, but those who find peace move forward despite the fear. Search within to avoid being paralyzed by fear.

April 24

Many survivors developed a hyper-fear response early on. Some of us have lived with it for so long that we do not know when we are fearful or calm. We just stopped paying attention. Thankfully, you can bring your fear response into better balance by finding a time or place when you feel quite relaxed and calm. Notice every sensation in your body. Your eyebrows are completely relaxed and so are your eyelids, even if your eyes are open. There are no imposed wrinkles in your face because it is completely calm. Your feet feel light, and you can even feel the blood running through them. Your shoulders may be erect or slouched, but they are not tight. Your head is held in place effortlessly by your neck. Your mind is at ease. Maybe you are sitting with your child, curled up with your favorite book, running on the treadmill or through the streets, or just lying in bed to drift off to sleep. Try to catch yourself with the feeling of being at peace and unafraid. Capture that moment. Capture it every chance you get until you are so familiar with it that you are creating it.

April 25

There are three peculiar reasons why adult survivors of childhood sexual abuse are more likely to be obese than the general population. First, our bodies often manifest what our minds feel. Survivors can feel so weighted down that their bodies manifest the weight perceived by the mind. Second, American culture associates beauty and sexuality with thinness. Since many survivors wish to downplay or completely reject sexuality, they prefer obesity. They may consciously or unconsciously try to hide sexuality with extra weight. Third, many survivors live outside of their bodies. They are out of touch with their bodies. So they do not pay attention to what they eat or what their bodies feel. They eat as a distraction rather than for nutrition. They also do not look in mirrors, do not exercise, and they may rarely buy clothing or wear make-up. They relate to their body in a basic way, mostly to carry their heads around. A survivor may have one or all three of these relationships with weight that may be a challenge on the healing path. Healing should reconnect the mind and body in a healthy way. Make sure you give yourself permission to invest in your beauty, health and sexuality as you heal.

April 26

Living as an adult survivor of childhood trauma is complex. There is the lack of memory, the inability to process what you do remember from a child's perspective, the behaviors that were developed to deal with the dysfunction, and much more. Survivor of childhood sexual abuse issues remain fundamentally misunderstood because we have been silent for so long. Most survivors do not understand their feelings and experiences. Therefore, do not expect loved ones to understand what you are still experiencing on the inside. The understanding of others cannot be a requirement for healing. We must learn to move forward by being proactive in our healing. The time has come for us to dive into the complexity of healing ourselves.

April 27

If we only had all bad memories of the family who hurt us, letting them go or putting distance between them and us would be easy. But the truth is that we give up a lot of good times and social benefits when we finally choose ourselves over family. So it does not feel right. It feels lonely, mean-spirited, selfish and even unnecessary to remove yourself from an environment where people love you. But each time you are in that environment you must pretend like you were never hurt because no one in that environment will allow you to speak. That is the cost of their love. It is not unconditional. You are trying to extend unconditional love to people who cannot extend it in return. The condition for their love is your silence. You have to choose to heal or choose to love (others) knowing that your love is not authentically you. When you choose to heal, you choose to love yourself, authentically.

April 28

The physical distance you create between yourself and your experience of childhood sexual abuse may make a difference in healing. That includes people, places, and things. If you are living in the house with elders who still request your silence, sharing family events with the violator, and frequenting the places of your youth where you were violated, for example attending the same church, then you are maintaining close emotional ties with the experience of abuse. If you are raising your children around the same people and places that hurt you, then healing is even more difficult. Unfortunately, these may be unavoidable situations at times, but survivors may maintain these bonds out of fear as well. Consider the possibility of creating more physical space to create safe space for yourself to heal. It may not happen immediately, but it will happen much sooner if you intentionally plan for it.

April 29

If you are waiting for validation of your pain from a specific person, then you are climbing in the box. If you are looking for someone to love you when you state that you do not love yourself, then you are putting the lid on the box. If you give up on healing because it is too much work, then you seal the box. No wonder you feel like you are suffocating instead of surviving. There is only room enough for one inside of your box, and the air is not good in there. But push just slightly and the lid will come right off. Just keep growing and the box will split right open, because it is not strong enough to hold you. You were not born in a box, and you certainly do not have to live in a box. Self-love, self-perseverance, and self-validation are important practices of healing. We practice daily, so we do not fit in a box.

April 30

When the world tells survivors not to cry, we must give ourselves permission to cry. When the world tells us to act like an adult now, we should honor our inner child. When the world tells us to shut up to avoid shame, we should break the silence to show strength. When the world tells us to put the abuse behind us, we have to give ourselves permission to be present in its pain. When the world tells us that we need to forgive our violators, we should forgive ourselves. Forgive ourselves for having taken the world's bad advice for so long. Let the healing begin.

5: SHOES ON THE WRONG FEET

Finding true love for self is far more important than finding true love in a partner. When you love from within, you will find love everywhere and anywhere. When you learn to partner with the universe, finding a partner to journey with you will be easier.

May 1

Healing sometimes interferes with our daily living. We do not necessarily need medicine or therapy or protection. Sometimes we are just letting the junk pass through us because we are not afraid of it anymore. You think healing is about gaining control of your life, but it is about surrender. You think it is about stopping the hurt, but it is about sitting with the pain. You think it is about being normal, but it is about being authentic. You think healing will fix your relationships, but it will show you whether your relationships are worth fixing. You think it will help you hold on, but it will teach you when to let go. You think healing is a destination, but it is a journey.

May 2

Well-meaning doctors may suggest medication to help survivors deal with the pain. They often have no idea how to sit with our pain or allow us to sit with our pain. Sometimes doctors are afraid of our pain just as much as our families, the violators, and our friends. They respond as if the pain is new and there is an urgency to stop it. However, the pain is not new, only the visibility of it is new. We have thought many times about 'not being here.' We have carried anxiety in our bodies from worrying about relationships and trying to make ourselves lovable for a long time. We have turned away from the mirror with self-hate often. Now that we are on the healing path we live instead of hide.

May 3

As survivors walk the healing journey, some of the right people will show up. They may show up and stay just long enough to move you to the next stage of healing, and then leave. There will be others who will keep coming back. Every time they leave you can count on them to eventually come back and give more. What both of these people do not realize is that as survivors we often settle for what we can get. But what helps us most is that person who showed up before they even knew what we were going through and stayed the whole time, through all the ups and downs and healing drama. These are the ones who are the most difficult to find.

May 4

We cannot keep looking at the world each day and expecting it to give us something different than what it gave us yesterday. Families, the media, doctors, friends, and co-workers are likely to offer us the same response on any given day. Our healing cannot rely on a shift in the external world. The external world changes much slower than our inner world. There are many areas of self that we can change instead of passively waiting for the world to change. Self-love, self-reflection, self-talk, self-affirmation, and self-knowledge are all important areas of change that we can control.

May 5

Survivors may find themselves in poor relationships because they relinquish personal power to try to control friendships. There is often a dysfunctional and unconscious interest in collecting people. Survivors often meet people and immediately begin to invest in fixing up the relationship so that the person will stay. They offer the person an enormous amount of space, money, time, attention or intimacy to make them happy. Survivors may use this relationship approach to avoid abandonment. It appears logical, but it is dysfunctional because the only people who need an enormous amount of space, money, time, attention, or intimacy to stay in someone's life is another person who operates from a place of dysfunction. Trauma often attracts trauma. So someone operating from a place of dysfunction may take everything that you have to offer. The problem is that they cannot give it back. They cannot give it back because they use it all. They leave nothing to share. They are not sharing life with you; they are taking life from you. Healthy people are more likely to reject an offering of someone giving up so much power to accommodate them. A healthy person does not take power or control from others, and they are likely to interpret the offer as an attempt to make them responsible for the other person's happiness. You will not attract healthy people with the routine of giving up your personal power. We should enter relationships knowing that we are enough, and let them unfold naturally rather than trying to manipulate people into staying by rendering our control to them.

May 6

We have to give ourselves permission to heal. There may be a tiny (or large) part of us that does not want to heal, that does not want to live well. For if we live well, there is no evidence of the crime. We carry the pain as evidence that horrific events have taken place without justice ever being served. But the time has come to heal. We can use our voice instead of the pain to reveal the chronicles of betrayal and dysfunction. We use our words, not only to speak like "Talking Trees," but to roar like rolling thunder that prepares the clouds to release their tears so that the trees will grow.

May 7

We are all involved in the healing process. However, just because we are involved in the healing process, does not mean we are healing. I can go to all of the financial investment seminars that I want, and say that I am involved in finances, but that will not make me rich. At some point, I have to determine my tolerance for financial risk and then take action that I hope will put me on the road to financial success. Similarly, effort and action are required for healing. At some point, you have to determine your tolerance for risk and take some action that may put you on the road to internal peace. What risks have you taken to move forward in your healing? What are you doing differently now that you are on the healing path? These are questions that we should ask ourselves frequently.

May 8

Some adult survivors of childhood sexual abuse have never had consensual sex, even as adults. Many survivors deny sexual pleasure and only engage in sex that victimizes. These survivors may only have sex to please a partner. They may not say yes or no to sex. Instead, they remain silent and follow the patterns of intimacy that developed during the abuse. Even as adults sexual consent must cover several issues. Both parties must agree to physical intimacy. No one can assume that physical intimacy is going to take place without asking for consent. As intimacy progresses, consent should continue to be sought. It is perfectly fine to limit the degree of physical contact. Both partners also have the right to request and use protection from unwanted pregnancy and disease. No one should progress with intercourse without giving the partner time to consider protection. Remember that it acceptable to kiss without advancing to intercourse. Requesting the use of a condom or another form of protection from unwanted pregnancy and disease is good self-care. It is also important to ask your partner to stop any time you become uncomfortable. A loving partner plays by your rules of "safety" rather than their need for sexual gratification.

May 9

Mother's Day is just around the corner. There are many survivors who have joyful memories to celebrate on Mother's Day, and to you, I say Happy Mother's Day. But most survivors have experienced dysfunctional childhoods and, at best, grew up with a fictionalized version of our family in our head, while our hearts hurt. Many of us had mothers who were too demanding, abusive, distant, and neglectful, or absent altogether. The emotionally absent mother left many survivors vulnerable to adverse childhood experiences that included, but were not limited to sexual abuse. We are still paying the price as we struggle, and often fail, to build healthy relationships with our children, spouses and friends while we continue to carry feelings of never being enough. To you, I say, you are enough. We are doing the best we can with what we were given. We are better today than we were yesterday. So on each Mother's Day celebrate your survival and resilience.

May 10

Forgiveness of violators is not required for healing. Forgiveness is an experience that may or may not arise at some point on the healing path for some survivors. However, it is neither necessary nor sufficient for survivors to reclaim their lives and live fully. Forced forgiveness of the violator is more damaging than no forgiveness. When you know you are not willing to forgive, you are giving yourself permission to live authentically. You are living in your truth. When you forgive violators for the sake of getting along with others, you are living someone else's lie instead of your truth.

May 11

Relationships that are toxic tear you down from the inside out. They typically bring out the worst in you in every aspect. Toxic people often (not always) require the use of drugs or alcohol to socialize, as well as encourage other illicit behavior such as infidelity or promiscuity. The relationship with a toxic person often carries some threat, such as withdrawing finances, attention, shared relationships or sex to disrupt your livelihood. Meanwhile, toxic people take as much as possible but are never satisfied. There is no satisfying a toxic person. Many survivors find themselves in these relationships because even abusive attention feels better than no attention at all to many people. You have to remember that healing is not about having attention. Healing is about attending to yourself. Attending to your internal self helps you build equitable relationships that can allow you to grow.

May 12

Coming out of denial of the effects of the abuse helps us deal with the guilt and shame that we carry, but it also creates discomfort. All the hurt that comes up from stuffing feelings for decades, all the repressed memories that resurface through dreams and triggers and all of the vulnerability that comes up from feeling exposed are strong enough to make us wish for the days of denial. Feeling emotions usually results in a crying phase that can easily last a year or more while we sort through the mess that we avoided for decades. We cry in bed, we cry at work, we cry at movies (even if it is a comedy), we cry with friends, we cry with children, we cry until our head and heart hurt and our nose become stuffed. This tear-fest is what we call progress because you are finally grieving. Grieving is important to healing.

May 13

There is a myth that therapists or other people plant false memories in the minds of survivors. This topic has been thoroughly researched, and the percentage of "false memories" accounts for only one percent to three percent of cases. What does happen more frequently is a distortion in the memory recall. The memory is connected to the events that surround it. So we often get details wrong depending on the context of the abuse. Maybe it was the aunt and not the uncle. Maybe it was your father and not your neighbor. Maybe you were age four instead of six. Maybe you told right away and were instructed to forget about it. It is much more likely that survivors repress memories than report false memories of sexual abuse. There are several reasons people forget or report inaccuracies. They may include: (1) The trauma was too much for the brain to process, which might suggest the survivor was forcibly raped and not groomed. (2) The abuse could have been initiated at an age too young to remember and stopped before memory was solidified. (3) Well-groomed victims may become so comfortable that their minds never process the sexual abuse. They grow up believing only in the goodness of the violator. If your adult mind is processing abuse issues, it is more likely that you are a survivor of childhood sexual abuse than you are creating false memories. You may be likely to create inaccurate memories, but not false memories. So give yourself full permission to heal.

May 14

Of course, we have moved on with our lives. That is what happens when you stay alive. Unfortunately, the pain moves with us. It moves with us from childhood to adulthood, from the old house to the new house, from the first job to the second job, from the sexual abuse to the consensual sex, from one relationship to the next, and even through numerous prescriptions. Moving on is not the same growth as healing. As we heal, we need vocabulary, concepts and theories that help us to understand what happened because no one ever told us or allowed us to tell them. We need encouragement and support because those who made it without the deep scars did not come back to tell us how to make it there too. We need listeners to believe us because our silence has been deafening. The question is whether others are capable of sitting with a survivor in the presence of pain.

May 15

Some pain needs to be revisited so that you can see it clearly now that you are better equipped to deal with it. No one can tell you when you should "move on." There is no time constraint on pain and trauma. You visit with the pain when it knocks on your door. You invite it in and ask what can it teach you about yourself today? The answer will often surprise you when you listen.

MAY 16

Are you asking "how do I heal" because you are prepared to do the work to heal, or are you asking the question as a defense mechanism? Is it a representation of doubt, fear and resistance? The first real step to healing could be releasing the need to know how to heal. Just commit to healing by any means necessary. Instead of repeating the question over and over in vain, repeat the statement "I'm committed to healing today." Carry this affirmation of responsibility in your heart each day. "Today, and every day, I commit myself to healing from within. I know that the answers I seek lie within me, so there is where I will seek and explore. I call back my energy from all of the sources I have allowed to absorb it from me. I will meet myself each day with love and acceptance, knowing that I am enough. I know that the darkness represents the untruths I have accepted, so I need not fear them. There is plenty of light in me to thrive."

MAY 17

Healing is not one size fits all. Every cough should not be treated like a cold. The remedy for a cold is drinking honey and lemon. But what if a cough is pneumonia, asthma, COPD or lung disease and you keep giving the person honey and lemon? Supporting a person on the healing journey requires a willingness to hear the symptoms and explore possible causes before telling them what to do. There is no formula for healing, just ideas, concepts, and information. How each person applies them will depend on the symptoms and circumstances. A 25-year-old healing is going to look differently than a 55-year-old healing. Someone molested by a coach may heal differently than an incest survivor. Someone living in poverty may heal differently than someone living in wealth. A male healing may look different from a female healing. Healing in Asian culture may look different from healing in North America. There are too many factors to assume that we know exactly what healing should look like for an individual. But we do know that all survivors deserve to be supported in their healing.

May 18

No one makes it through life without challenges. Childhood trauma, however, means that we have to apply adult problem solving before we have even developed the mental resources to do so. Consequently, we come into adulthood with an altered reality of ourselves and the world. Moreover, we still do not get excused from the normal challenges of adult life just because our challenges started in childhood. It means we have to always work harder to create and maintain quality mental health.

May 19

We have to be careful not to spend more time and energy trying to fix others (like our children, spouses, or friends or the world) that we ignore our healing. It is tempting to point out flaws in others when our flaws are too difficult to face. When we find ourselves in deep pain or constant conflict, we deserve a moment to self-reflect. When it is the case that people are toxic, then we have a responsibility to divest in the relationship rather than invest. We do not have a responsibility to fix people so that we can remain in relationships with them. That may mean that we will be left alone to deal with our pain.

May 20

We cannot heal ourselves by investing in healing our relationships. It works the other way around. When we heal ourselves, we heal our relationships. We have to address the trauma response within us that keeps us clinging to relationships in the hope of healing. We must address our feelings of insignificance. Sometimes if we can identify the exact source(s) of the pain, we can rewrite our perception of history. No, we cannot go back and relive it, but we can rewrite it. You rewrite it in your mind because that is where the pain is lodged. You can touch the pain, face it, embrace it, and wrap your arms all around it. Feel it fully, once and for all. Only then can you step in and create a new script that will enable us to heal our relationships.

May 21

We often have expectations of people based on our pain as if they are not carrying baggage already. We exist in a world full of people who are hurting instead of people who are healing. The real opportunity for adult survivors of childhood sexual abuse is that we can collectively change the way people deal with pain. We get to create a model for the world that says silence is not a solution to pain. We get to be the leaders. We have earned the right, and we can own the responsibility to be the change that we want to see in the world.

May 22

Obviously, no one would choose to experience life as a survivor of childhood sexual abuse. However, we know that no one gets through life without challenges or tragedy along the way. There are many survivors of childhood trauma, including emotional abuse and neglect, early loss of parents, physical abuse, incarceration and mental illness. Most survivors hide instead of heal their pain. Adult survivors of childhood sexual abuse can have an impact on humanity by creating safe space for healing. As we heal from our pain and trauma, we give all survivors permission and motivation to do the same.

May 23

Be a seeker of truth, not comfort. The truth will eventually set you free. Comfort is more likely to imprison you. When you have lived a life of pain, seeking comfort makes sense. However, comfort may also breed attachment and addiction, to people, not just substances. It rarely leads to truth. The truth may bear a lot of pain, but eventually, comfort comes. Seeking truth is like planting seeds in fertile ground. Beauty is going to grow as long as you take care of the space where you have sown the seeds. Seeking comfort is more like purchasing a dozen roses from the flower shop. They are beautiful and extraordinary. But they will not last long. The longer you have them, the less beautiful they become as they wilt and die. You can hold on to them, even freeze them for a memento, but they will never beautifully display again. Are you going to dig into the dirt to plant your flowers or are you going to continue to shop at the florist?

May 24

Even if we feel wounded forever, we do not have to live a life that is dictated by our wounds. We can still make good choices about the way we live. We can pay attention to our body, mind and heart. Even if we cannot hold the peace as long as we like, we can learn to spend more time in a state of peace. Even if we never have long-term relationships, we can grow from each interaction that we have with people in our lives. Healing is a journey without a destination. We can live from a place of healing, rather react from a place of pain.

May 25

Psychology calls it growth mindset. Education calls it self-efficacy. Religion calls it faith. Social work calls it resilience. Medicine calls it optimism and journalists call it a positive outlook. "It" is the use of mental energy to influence the outcome of given situations. The more distressful the situation, the more important "it" is. Life is interactive. We bring energy to every event and experience in our life. The energy we bring can negatively or positively influence (not control) the outcome. This energy is initiated "within." So check within to make sure you are not negatively charged before you initiate your external response. Create responses that move you forward instead of reactions that hold you back.

May 26

You can heal yourself. In fact, you are the only one that can heal you. But you cannot heal without proper tools. Important tools for healing are knowledge, inspiration, support network, tolerance for risks, forgiveness, readiness to change and an open heart. Healing is the best do it yourself project there is.

May 27

When you have given 100% of what you can give, rest your mind and wait for a response from the universe. Our minds are so limited in comparison to the energy that the universe can bring to our lives. Possibilities are endless. Obstacles can be removed, or we can be given the strength to endure. When we work for change and healing in our lives we do not know what it will look like. Look for the yes that the universe responds with, rather than the "no" that you feel when you notice what is missing.

May 28

If you are feeling stuck in your healing, these are some questions to ponder. Are you working on healing, or just hoping to be healed? Are you going to the therapist to feel good, or to do the work that sometimes feel painful? Are you reading through the websites just to confirm that you are not crazy, or are you applying the advice to become sane? Are you interested in understanding yourself as a complete human being, or are you only attached to your identity as a survivor of childhood sexual abuse? Be honest with yourself. Wherever you are on the path is fine as long as you remain conscious of your progress and growth.

May 29

Paying attention to our bodies is important because many of us feel betrayed by our bodies and emotionally detach from it as a response. Sometimes it is this emotional detachment from our bodies that cause physical illness, obesity or premature aging. Our bodies did not betray us; people betrayed us. Do not take it out on your body. Your body should be beautiful, healthy and ageless, unapologetically. It can also give and receive pleasure shamelessly. But we have to pay attention to it and love it.

May 30

The brain prefers to respond with "yes" instead of "no." The brain is biased toward the idea of accumulation and resists the idea of loss. Stopping negative behaviors, such as overeating or drinking, is extremely difficult because stopping equals a loss to the brain. The brain panics over the idea of loss or deprivation. Healing should focus on positive interests that allow you to say yes. Say yes to loving yourself, taking care of your body, finding your voice, letting go of fear, and taking risks to move forward. Say yes to good nutrition, exercise, and meditation. Say yes to education, taking a vacation, or finding a new job. Find the "yes" in your life. Your spirit will thank you.

May 31

Your choice is to honor your truth or pretend like your truth does not matter. It is a difficult decision to honor yourself when you know that the consequence will be that you are alone, without friends or family. But when you do honor your truth (only if necessary), good people will eventually show up to keep you company. Healthy people will typically steer clear of environments that are messy because they value themselves too much. So when you keep making room in your life for the messy folks, then the clutter will not leave room for the type of people you want to show up in your life. Creating safe space for yourself will invite safe people into your life.

6: FETAL POSITION

If there is no communication, awareness or recognition between the inner child and the adult self, then it is difficult for the adult brain to stop destructive patterns. The inner child may act out the childhood patterns of dysfunction, and the adult continues to get disappointed.

June 1

Breaking the silence is not a single action to be done. It starts in the mind before anyone can see it. Mentally, we must let go of the arrangement to put ourselves last and put the protection of others first. We have to let go of the vow of secrecy to never admit we were sexually abused. We have to tell ourselves the truth about the misconduct of adults during our childhood. Breaking the denial in our mind comes before breaking the silence with our voice. We must first accept the truth. How we publicly deal with our truth depends on our age and dependency on family members, personal resources, support system and ultimately our comfort. We are not required to ever disclose details about our abuse, whether we choose to speak publicly or privately. Breaking the silence is about letting go of the secret. The details are not what is protecting the violator. Hiding the fact that we are survivors protects all violators. Breaking the silence is part of breaking the cycle of victimization.

June 2

Understand that our urge to heal our present is what beckons us to return to the past. We are now capable of doing what we could not do as children. We are capable of mature evaluation and assessment of those who violated us. We are capable of reflecting on our living environments and circumstances that contributed to our vulnerability. The reason it is so important now is because we could not do it then. No matter how difficult the consequences of our healing may be now, we know that we could not even process and deal with it when we were children. We now try to follow the tracks of our tears so that we can understand how we came to be here.

June 3

I bet many of us have at least contemplated meeting with family members after a period of no contact. There is no right approach except to follow your heart. Let me offer these considerations nevertheless: 1) You get to be angry and distant for as long as you like. Healing is not about getting rid of the anger. It is about managing your life. Some of us have to learn to manage life despite the anger. 2) On the other hand, being angry is not a requirement for being a survivor. You can allow your anger to dissipate as you heal. There is no need to hold onto it when life takes you to a place of resolve. Accept resolve over anger and know that you no longer need it to protect yourself. 3) No matter what happens in the meeting you get to decide the direction of your life. You do not have to continue meeting or extend any relationship. 4) Your family member was a victim too. They did what they knew to do. It may have been wrong and hurtful. But do not expect them to apologize for it or even acknowledge it because the chances are that they are still victims. You may set yourself up for triggers if you meet them with expectations. If you are willing to forgive, that is great. But do not set yourself up by assuming they are seeking forgiveness. Meeting represents your growth and healing, not theirs.

June 4

Many survivors lose memories of actual events, making accounts of what happened easy to dismiss. But you do not need memories of actual events to give yourself permission to heal. You do not need to prove or convince anyone that you were violated. In general, the worse the abuse was for the victim, the more likely memory repression is to occur. So if you cannot remember the abuse, then the abuse is likely to have been worse than you imagine, rather than being insignificant. But you do not need memory to journey on the healing path.

June 5

Silence should offer you peace, rather than anxiety. Silent space should offer a reflection on purpose and progress. It should not arise in you fear of isolation and abandonment. It does not matter if you are in the presence of someone you love, in a conversation with a stranger, working at your desk, driving in the car, falling asleep or doing chores. Welcome silence and welcome yourself. If you are afraid of silence, then you should confront your fear by adding more silence instead of adding more distraction.

June 6

There are two places that we can look for significance, internally and externally. When we look for external significance we rely on others to show us that we are important. The outside world changes our internal world. When people tell us we are important, we feel important. If they do not show us that we are important, we do not feel important. The other place to look is inside ourselves. We feel self-acceptance. Like trees, we feed on the sun to connect to the universe. No one waters a tree for it to grow. It is grounded and rooted so deep in the universe that it grows through its participation with the earth. It does change with the seasons, but it never forgets its significance. Likewise, when we ground ourselves in the universe, we never forget our significance. Moreover, when we recognize our internal significance, we change the external world. What are you significant enough to do?

June 7

Try to not be intimidated by the newness of your life as you heal. Healing brings new energy into your life. It could be in the form of friendship, job, new activities, travel, or an old opportunity that you once passed up because of fear. The new energy in our life may take us out of our comfort zone. Just remember that comfort usually only means familiar. It does not tell us what is right or necessary. Feel the energy and let it move you into that new space. Those that you have relied upon may not like that new space. So the new energy may take people and things out of your life as well as bring them in. Your task is to pay attention and embrace it.

June 8

Breaking the silence might require us to break the contracts that we have in our heads about family and love. Interestingly, we do not require that family hold up their end of the bargain about the ideal family. We only require it of ourselves. Our idealized concept of family and love was broken when incest was ignored or supported. When we were not protected as children or believed and supported in our healing as adults, the myth of the perfect family died. Maybe it is time to stop fighting and sacrificing for what does not exist.

June 9

Something brought you to this place of healing. Whatever it was, know that it will move you forward as well. Even if pain brought you here, there had to be hope attached to the pain for you to end up on the healing path. There is no mistake that you belong here. Listen to your heart, open your eyes, speak your mind, feel your joy. Live your best life. Being a survivor does not have to take away any of the ability to do so, but being a victim does. You are no longer a victim. You are a survivor trying to thrive instead of dying. Trust that whatever brought you to this place of healing will continue to hold you until all of the possibilities are back in your life.

June 10

All you wanted was to be believed. You were not attempting to break up a family. You were not seeking attention. You were seeking support from those who claimed to love you as you finally bring forth your truth. You are a human being, worthy of being loved and honored. You are an adult who is capable of thinking, choosing, and changing according to what you know to be in your best interest at the time, not according to how happy you make other people. You are a spirit, bruised, but not broken, connected to The Spirit and grounded in humanity even as you heal. You have finally chosen the healing path and will stand fast on it whether you are walking, running or crawling. At least, you are on it. Your healing is not about other people and the choices that they make or the consequences their past actions bring them. You have found the healing path because you knew you were worthy of healing.

June 11

If something matters, then the presence of it will create a change in your experience. Likewise, its absence will create a change in your experience. The problem is that everything that matters to us, we make significant. We do not have to do so, nor should we. Some things that are significant we should not allow to matter. A person's job is significant, but it should not matter that much because it is just one of many ways to manage our lifestyle. There are other means one can use to bring prosperity. Healing from trauma allows us to make the abuse experience matter less, even though it will always be significant. The absence of a normal childhood created a negative change in the internal experience of the survivor. As we heal, that internal drive shifts back in the direction of normal. Although the abuse memories can never go away, the experience matters less and less as an influence in our lives.

June 12

The purpose of disclosure is to live authentically, but there are many issues that arise after disclosure. You may wonder how to live openly with the abuse that you want to forget. You may be disappointed that no one comes to save you now that people know your pain. You may feel more isolated because people who say they want to listen, cannot hear what you try to express. You have to figure out how to fill the void of the broken relationships with people who shy away from our pain. None of these issues resolve themselves no matter how much detail about the abuse you disclose. You have to explore how the guilt, shame, anger, fear, hyper-alertness and mistrust manifest themselves through your choices and responses to the world. Ask yourself what is your relationship with people, yourself and the world as a consequence of the abuse, and then address what you find.

June 13

The healing journey is not a race. It is a way of living. There is no destination and no road map. But fear not, for you are not alone. We travel together though sometimes taking different paths at the forks in the road. Some travel slowly, others fast. Some rest frequently, and some do not rest at all. Some of us travel in luxury automobiles, and some of us travel on bikes. But for all of us, there are signposts along the path that we should learn how to read, like dangerous curve ahead, yield, one-way traffic, toll road, and carpool lane only. Pay attention to the signs.

June 14

Healthy child development depends on eighteen years of healthy childhood experiences. That does not mean that a child will not have some ups and downs and common struggles, but caring adults should help children navigate life's challenges to help them avoid unnecessary struggles. They are not supposed to willingly impose trauma or stagnate development. Adult survivors of childhood trauma often fail to consider the environment that put them at risk for abuse. The absence of reliable, accessible, trusting, and caring adults in the life of a child increases the likelihood of adverse experiences. When we look at how the violator gained access to us as children, we will uncover another layer of healing that needs to be done. Sometimes the environment that gave violators access to victims is a bigger challenge to healing than the abuse itself.

June 15

Pain means that sorrow has arrived, so rejecting it will not make it vanish. We can run from it, but it knows our destination. So as soon as we slow down it greets us again. We can ignore it, but that will not diffuse it. Pain is like an infection; it will spread throughout our lives if we ignore it. So what is left? Embrace it. Use it as a guide to reveal secrets of your inner self. Follow it, instead of just running from it. Give it your attention and let it heal your whole life.

June 16

There is pain in silence, and there is pain in breaking the silence. Keeping it in hurts and letting it out hurts. But the pain of silence is not the same as the pain of healing. Silence takes you down a lonely path of self-destruction, internally or externally. Healing, though painful, leads to living at a higher vibration. Not only are you empowering yourself, but you are also empowering others. In silence, you suffer alone. In breaking the silence you grow with others.

June 17

Sometimes we are burdened down by the baggage we try to carry on the healing path. Traveling the path is difficult when we carry heavy loads. There will be lots of baggage that you will have to let go of on the healing path. Carrying baggage will never make you stronger. To be stronger, you have to carry less weight. Lighten a load of guilt on your mind. Lighten the worry about the future. Lighten the fear of being abandoned. Lighten the demands of emotionally crippling relationships. Lighten the clinging to useless identities. All of this baggage weighs you down. When we get rid of unnecessary baggage, relationships, careers, and favorite materialism may go as well. This purging is a natural part of the healing process.

June 18

We don't move forward by letting go of the past. Have you ever tried to pull out of a tight parking space by putting your foot on the gas? No! The tighter the parking space, the more times you have to back up before you can turn the wheels enough to get out. Similarly, the smaller you have made your life in order to remain parked in your favorite spot, the more you will have to return to your past. You inch away from the past to avoid careless damage to the things around you. But you must go in reverse. You must turn your head fully and stretch that neck to get a good look to assess what is behind you.

June 19

As we uncover the pieces of the puzzle to heal, there are a few common pieces that survivors often share. First, we often come to find out that the secret was not a secret after all. There was someone else that knew what happened to you and never spoke about it. Second, the person who violated you also violated others close to you, but neither of you ever spoke about it. Third, we often find out that there were several violators in the family, not just one. Other relatives were violated by the other violators who may never have touched you. We often find out that incest was not the only family secret. There was more dysfunction than we ever realized. Every piece we turn over brings us more pain and more understanding at the same time.

June 20

Some days we play tug of war with our hearts and minds. We know we are phenomenal because we survived and we are thriving to tell about it. We smile at the thought of our greatness, right before we put the dagger into our own hearts with self-criticism of not being where we want to be, for making the same mistakes over and over, or for not feeling adequate. Yes, love and hate can coexist. Which thought will win on any given day is the thought that you feed. Acknowledge all of the negative thoughts when they arise, but embrace the positive ones and multiply them. That is how we win at tug of war.

June 21

If it is possible to still love and respect those who were directly or indirectly involved in your abuse without making yourself small, then you are in a great space. However, if you have committed to loving those who hurt you at the expense of not loving yourself, then you are likely to still be in denial. Making yourself insignificant and ignoring your needs is not a requirement for love. Love should not come at a sacrifice of oneself. That is the lie we were taught as children. You can let it go now. You do not have to hold onto relationships that hurt you. Commit to your healing before you commit to relationships. Those that need to be in your life will remain.

June 22

Today is moving day; every day is moving day. Move forward into consciousness. Train your mind to recognize memories as pictures of the past, and not the current reality. When memories of the abuse trigger pain or fear or anger, remind yourself that it is only a memory. It does not dictate your present reality. You may be able to put those pictures away by using a mantra, such as, "today is the most important day of my life. I will be present in it." You can say that (or something like that) every time your mind takes you somewhere that disturbs you. Use it 100 times a day if necessary. Follow the mantra back to the present moment. You must be willing to immediately let go of the disturbing thought once you speak the mantra. If you are alone, say the mantra aloud. If not, try to whisper it. If you are engaged in conversation with someone, then say it to yourself in your head. It works, but it takes a lot of practice.

June 23

If you think that surviving childhood sexual abuse has made you a stronger person, then you have yet to find your true strength. The truth is that being a survivor makes us more vulnerable to addiction, abusive relationships, psychological and physical disorders, self-harm, and participation in illegal activity. Adult survivors of childhood sexual abuse are over-represented in all of these categories. The abuse did not make us stronger than we were or stronger than we would have been. That myth enables people to dismiss our pain. People grow into their fullest potential when they have support to take safe risks, safety nets to make mistakes, encouragement to move forward and love to stabilize them. Healing builds this potential back into our lives through our resilience.

June 24

The commitment to healing yourself works better if it is approached with a commitment to healing the universe. Healing the universe works a whole lot better if it is a commitment to healing yourself. The two commitments work hand in hand because we interact with the universe. The energy you release toward the universe plays a role in your healing. It is sort of like the universe is your boss. Most of us report to work each week for a large number of hours to make someone else successful, fulfill someone else's dream, or make someone else look good. Hopefully, you have a job that you enjoy, and you do not just go about your job completely without enthusiasm. However, you invest your time into this job because you realize that working for someone is related to your vitality. You get to eat, have material possessions to take care of yourself and raise children. Those who succeed in their work make a positive contribution to the work environment as well as help the company to reach its goal. Well, the universe is everybody's boss, and all the people are our co-workers. Each day we contribute to the work environment, and we have the opportunity for promotion based on our efforts to move humanity forward. When we live this way, we are more likely to move from being a survivor to thriving.

June 25

As children, we endured a horrible physical and emotional captivity of irresponsible and ill adults. But we survived. Unfortunately, many of us remain captives of our own minds as adults. That may even be worse torture. Self-doubt and self-hate, negative thinking, and lack of discipline and motivation are all ingredients for emotional torture that you will not grow out of. You break free of your mind by "watching" what is going on up there. When you say, "I hate myself," I and myself are separate entities. "I" is doing the feeling and "myself" is doing the reporting. There is a shift that will happen if you change "myself" from being the reporter to being the watcher. The watcher "watches" and knows that what it sees is not the real "self," because the watcher is the real self. So when the "I hate myself" comes up again, the watcher does not record it for playback. It only watches. This practice begins the transformation of the mind.

June 26

If only you could remember what it was like to be a toddler learning how to walk, how many times you fell and got back up. If only you could remember what it felt like to learn how to read, people always correcting the words you read wrong. If only you could remember what it was like to learn how to ride a bike, the risk of falling you took. If only you could remember what it was like to learn how to swim, going in the deep water that was over your head, where your feet did not touch the bottom anymore. You probably have forgotten the fear in which you approached these tasks. We are equipped to handle the difficult survival tasks of life, including healing. You do not have to stop being afraid. You just have to commit to moving despite the fear.

June 27

Part of the difficulty of healing is that we have been unhealthy most of our lives, especially since abuse typically occurs in families that are dysfunctional. The average onset of childhood sexual abuse is during the elementary school years, too young to know what to expect from the world because our family is our world at that age. Since the world has never been "normal" for most of us, it is difficult to know how normal relationships with anyone operate. The best approach, then, is to commit to living in truth instead of trying to be normal. Seek truth. Ask for truth, and offer truth, even if it is painful, scary or isolating.

June 28

When a child does not have healthy attachments with loving adults, then later adult relationships can be compromised due to unrealistic expectations. Survivors have a tendency to approach relationships from a position of fear, which invites a lot of heaviness into the relationship. There is a fear of abandonment that compels survivors to sacrifice themselves for love in hope that a person will never leave. However, genuine love leaves the door open so that people can come and go as they need, rather than trying to persuade people to stay as a result of self-sacrifice. Obviously, the first love must be to oneself, but many survivors find it "easier" to try to persuade others to love them than to love themselves. That is a pattern of dysfunction that should be broken.

June 29

Aligning your life based on what you lack may make you depressed, lonely, or angry. When we live from a position of lack, there is a feeling of void. However, lack is usually a misperception. Healing requires recognition that there is no lack. When you feel the lie of lack, you have to refocus to see the reality of what is there. If you feel a lack of time with someone special, focus on what that free time may offer you. You could use the time to exercise, be with your children, meditate or read. You have likely left something unfulfilled in your life that requires you to have time, which you have perceived as a lack. Your perception that you lack time from a specific person distorts the opportunity for you to grow by using time differently in your life. Similarly, if you feel a lack of love, then ask yourself what you need to do to show love to yourself. If you have a lack of money, then you can focus on evaluating your lifestyle choices. These are just a few examples of how you can refocus whenever you feel a sense of lack.

June 30

The importance of being present is not just some spiritual or therapy mumbo jumbo that is impossible to do. It is an important psychological concept that circumvents the failure of thought suppression. Thought suppression is the act of trying not to act or think a certain way. In our case, it may be trying not to think about the abuse or trying not to feel so hurt about it. There is plenty of research that show us that trying to send messages to our brain to not do something has the exact opposite effect. In spiritual language, we advise that whatever we resist becomes stronger. So it is better to be present with whatever it is we are tempted to resist. Offer no resistance.

7: FAIRY TELLS

Tears often flow when we begin to live life authentically. We begin to release ourselves from our façade and begin to rebuild our spirit. Tears show strength, not weakness.

July 1

Do not be afraid to look at the "ugly" in you. That is part of healing. Ugly can be transformed. Healing is transformative work. We spend our lives chipping away the bricks, sanding off the rust, pulling up the weeds. There are days we step back and notice how much work there is left to do. Other days we step back and admire the progress. But most days we have to just keep plugging away. You should try your best not to become paralyzed by what lies ahead or complacent with what has been accomplished. The journey, the healing and the transformation last a lifetime.

July 2

Physical intimacy can be quite a challenge for survivors.

Sometimes survivors resort to physical intimacy without emotional attachment. Other survivors may shy away from physical intimacy and only prefer emotional attachment. Either of these situations may make it difficult to establish and maintain quality relationships. For the most part, physical intimacy is an important aspect of long-term partnering, and it should be satisfying to both partners. Communication is key as we determine our boundaries for physical intimacy. Communication is the best way to make sure that your consensual sexual contact does not trigger feelings of victimization. There are ways to distinguish between victimization and consent. Victims do not get to choose. You are now a participant. You can tell your partner when you are ready to be touched and how you want to be touched. Victims are not in control. You now get to be in control the entire time. You get to set the pace of the interaction by asking your partner to go slower or change directions. Most importantly, you get to say stop if you feel uncomfortable. The goal of sex should be for you to allow yourself to share pleasure with your partner rather than for you to give pleasure to your partner.

July 3

Once you accept that fact that healing, then it becomes within reach. You can say healing is difficult and use it as a reason to keep doing what is dysfunctional. Or you can state it as an awareness to prepare your mind for the journey with hope, determination, tenacity and persistence. Healing is difficult, not impossible. It is also natural, necessary and collective. You are ready and able to sustain the life-long journey.

July 4

A simple inventory of your life is to look at the people who you are drawing into it. If all of the people in your personal life rely heavily on you for their well-being, then you may be using them as a distraction from your pain. If all of the people in your life attempt to make you heavily dependent on them, then you may be using them as a scapegoat for your pain. One sign of growth is when you attract and develop healthy relationships that help you become a better person by supporting you and growing with you. If your relationships are not healthy, do not work on your relationship; work on yourself.

July 5

More often than not, survivors of childhood sexual abuse were raised in dysfunctional families. The sexual abuse was a symptom of the dysfunction rather than the cause of it. Drug abuse, mental illness, illegal activity, debilitating physical illness, or just poor parenting skills likely opened the door to victimization. We survived that environment. Now we are changing, but that environment in which the abuse took place is likely the same. If that environment supported violators when we were children, it is likely to support violators in adulthood. Unfortunately, when we decide that we can no longer tolerate an environment with known violators, we have to make the decision to leave. You are the one who suffered from the dysfunction then, and you are the one who will still suffer until you release yourself from the dysfunction.

July 6

There is no amount of love or care that anyone can offer you to make up for what you did not get as a child. You have the right and the need to mourn that loss, not replace it. When we stop seeking a replacement for our childhood loss, we may start healing within. Speak the truth that you could not speak as a child. Cry the tears that you could not cry as a child. Feel the pain you did not know you had a right to feel as a child. There is so much within you that needs to be healed. No one can take away your need to be healed, and no one can heal you but yourself. You are capable of healing no matter what your past has been.

July 7

In truth, you know at least some of the answer to the questions you ask about how to heal. You know the people, places and things you should stay away from to create your safe space. You know you need to exercise to take back your body and stimulate your brain. You know you need to read healthy material about healing. When these questions about healing arise in you, the answers arise with them, but most people resist the answers because they are not easy. They require action. If the question of "how" is seeking for a way to heal without making the tough changes in your life, then the answer is to let go of resistance. Let go of the idea that healing will make you feel better. Healing will not make you feel better. It will make you live better. Once you begin to live better, you will attract a whole different set of circumstance in your life.

July 8

Where there is pain, there is resistance, where there is resistance, there is pain. So if you feel the resistance, look for the pain. If you feel the pain, look for the resistance. We resist letting go of our illusions, the illusions of family, or love or support or even the illusion of happiness. We often hold onto the concept of how these constructs are supposed to look or make us feel, but that is not at all what we are getting out of them. We refuse to let them go or to accept them. Instead, we remain in a state of resistance, and resistance hurts because you are going against the grain. We invite growth and happiness when we look for the flow of energy and go with the flow. Allow experiences to pass through your life without trying to hold onto them as if they are what makes you you. Leave people space to enter and to exit your life according to your and their needs. Live with an open heart and mind, without resistance.

July 9

Dots of confusion, specks of fear, and pebbles of rejection filled the smallest cracks in the deepest hole that housed our soul before we arrived on the healing path. We had no idea what it felt like to matter in the world. We had made ourselves so small to fit into the tiny space denial. We yelled for help, but only silence was heard from the depth in which our mind was buried. Finally, we broke through the silence. We are ready to rise and roar like the lion. Now confusion grows into insight; fear transforms into audacity, and rejection evolves into discipline. We have begun a revolution of healing.

July 10

You are moving forward. Look at the moon and notice each night how it changes. Sometimes it is full, half, quarter. That does that mean the moon is going backward or shrinking. No, how big it is depends on its current position in relationship to the earth. The same goes for healing. How much growth you can observe at any given time always depends on your relationship to the particular situation. Whenever you see yourself as small, it does not mean that you are going backward, or that growth has stopped. It just means that you have a disadvantaged view.

July 11

Love became a twisted concept for many survivors when the

abuse was committed by the violator's misrepresentation of love that was used to manipulate. Consequently, many survivors were left with a distorted sense of love that encourages them to sacrifice themselves in the hope of earning and keeping a person's attention. They learn to give their love away. Giving away love is based on a distortion. Real love is shared in a relationship. If you give something to someone else, they can do whatever they please with it because once you give it away, it is no longer yours. You do not have any say in how it is handled. But when you share with someone, you must keep some for yourself. In the case of sharing love, you feast on it together, like a gourmet meal, watching each other take a delicious bite and getting full together. Healing makes us better lovers because it helps us to love ourselves so that we can share our love with others.

July 12

Giving Birth typically leaves stretch marks from being pregnant. For a long time, the mother carries a growing mass within her that eventually develops into an extension of self that is beautiful and wonderful with the potential to change the world. Likewise, survivors have stretch marks on our heart from carrying a mass of silence and grief for a long time. Breaking the silence is like giving birth. Our new voice must be nurtured for years as it turns into an extension of self that is wonderful and beautiful that can change the world.

July 13

No one can tell you how to heal. However, there are some common themes to taking back your life. When your life begins to feel like "your life," rather than just your existence, you have most likely developed self-regulation, autonomy, independence, self-efficacy, and competence. These characteristics are all similar, but not the same. You may develop more in one area than another, but you are likely to develop at least some in all of the areas as you heal. Autonomy is feeling comfortable tasks on your own and feeling fine when you are alone. You become better at organizing your daily life without a strong need for input from others. Independence is similar to autonomy. You explore new boundaries on your own, without approval or assistance of others. Self-regulation is the ability to monitor your progress, plan and predict your success. Efficacy is your positive belief in your ability to complete the task at hand. Efficacy is significantly related to the actual success a person achieves. Competence has to do with knowing how to set yourself up for successes. Failure is information that forces us to redirect. Failure is not bad. But the absence of success for long periods of times or trials may mean that we are weak in the other areas of autonomy, independence, self-regulation, and efficacy. The best news is that we all develop these qualities as we heal. Just consciously put them on your radar as growth patterns to pay attention to and watch for opportunities to practice and develop.

July 14

Some people believe incest only refers to sexual contact between people who are related by birth. More accurately, incest includes people related to one another by any close association, not just blood. Incestuous relationships include any members of the same household, any relatives by marriage and those related by adoption. It also includes all physically intimate contact initiated for the purpose of sexual stimulation, not just penetration. Incest cannot be consensual if one of the participants is under the legal age of consent or if one of the participants is coerced. Adult survivors of incest are the least likely to disclose childhood sexual abuse due to an even higher stigma and shame associated with the experience. We did not get to choose the violators. Obviously, we would have chosen not. All victims have a right to heal.

July 15

Taking control of our lives does not mean that we get to control the outcomes. It means that we get to control where we invest our energies. We can exert control by making choices. When we are uncomfortable we can make a conscious decision to control the situation. Action may need to be taken externally, meaning that you actively resolve the situation by making a decision, or internally, which means you work out your feelings about the situation. Either way, you only get to control your end of it. You cannot control anyone's response. You delay your healing when you try to control other people's response.

July 16

A unique experience of incest is that the victim has to share a part of their world with the violator. Even as adults, if the survivor wants the perpetrator out of her or his life, they often have to avoid the entire family. Even though family members may know about the past abuse, rarely do they demand or protect the desired physical distance between the violator and survivor. Consequently, the healing process is so slow. The survivor spends far too much time trying to find safe space so that they can heal. Safe space cannot be found as long as the survivor has to face the threat of sharing an environment with the violator. When the violator is a stranger, there is never an expectation for the victim to share space with the violator. Most people would do whatever they could to create space between victims and survivors. Unfortunately, the closer the relationship between the victim and violator, the less support victims tend to receive.

July 17

Some survivors have a deep fear of being alone, fear of not being loved, and fear of taking care of themselves. The general term is "fear of abandonment." People who suffer from this issue need constant distractions, affirmations, and attention from an outside source. Depending on the depth of the problem, they will try to maintain contact with people, including engaging people in arguments, engaging in sex, participating in harmful activities and giving people control over their lives. Fear of abandonment is a serious issue that most likely evolved from a failure to have attachment needs met as a child. It often requires the help of a professional to do inner child work.

July 18

Not only are families that sexually abuse children likely to have more than one violator, but they are also likely to have more than one victim, all silenced. Siblings may never know that they are both being abused by the grandfather. Children who share a Sunday school teacher may never know they have more in common than the required scripture. Children on the same team may be groomed to compete for the coach's "attention." Know that when you break your silence, the truth will unfold about the victimization you experienced, and you will clearly know that you are not to blame.

July 19

Survivors of childhood sexual abuse may experience post-traumatic stress disorder well into their adult years, even 50 years later. Symptoms include flashbacks, physical illness, depression, inability to maintain healthy relationships and frequent thoughts of suicide. Many survivors of childhood sexual abuse blame themselves for not being able to stop the abuse. This self-blame results in intense feelings of guilt and shame that prevent them from seeking help for post-traumatic stress symptoms. Survivors who keep their abuse a secret may suffer greater psychological distress than survivors who disclose the abuse. We could not prevent the abuse, but we can begin to heal even if it is 50 years later.

July 20

When forgiveness is goal-oriented, it is similar to losing weight by becoming anorexic. If you forgive the violator, but you cannot maintain healthy, positive relationships with your spouse or children, and then your investment in the healing process may be misdirected and unhealthy. Healing does not have to begin with forgiveness. Healing should focus on mastering your (internal and external) environment. Forgiveness is not part of the work. It is a consequence of the work. Forgiveness arises after you have done the work.

July 21

The core of who we are is not determined by our experience, but by our purpose. No one or no experience can keep you from your purpose. Your purpose is your healing power. When you discover why you are here, you will develop the power you need to serve. Pain, at different times, may direct us toward or away from our purpose. As we heal, we will know the difference. Of course, we want to move into our purpose. So we have to heal. As we heal, we move into our purpose. As we move into our purpose, we also heal.

July 22

Many of us have followed the road to success like a GPS navigator with turn by turn directions. We arrived at our destination with beautiful children, a good job, a quality education, a strong belief in God and one or two good friends. It is all that society told us matters. So we smile and wave as we continue to listen to the silent screams in our head that whispers, and then shouts. "There is no peace here." We thought the road to success would lead us to peace, and quiet the voices in our head. Instead, when we arrived, the voices awakened. The trauma came back to life. Your past collided with your present and threatened your future. The message is simple. It is time to heal. It is time to break the silence. You do not have to keep incest and childhood sexual abuse a secret. To do so keeps you intimately tied to the perpetrator and distant from your true self despite your success. Living openly may interrupt the life you built to bring you success, but that may not be bad. Your new life will focus on authenticity and transparency.

July 23

How many times you have failed is not important. Returning to old patterns that you know are self-destructive does not make you a failure. Even if you are stopped by fear, you are still on the healing path. Avoiding mistakes is not what makes us the great travelers on the path. What matters is your determination to get up and move forward from wherever you are today. Today is an opportunity for you to be better than you were yesterday. Do not waste it on regret.

July 24

Healing does not always come in a neat and tidy package. We are called to heal by any means necessary. Sometimes it is ugly and rude and forceful. We have to do the dirty work of healing. We have to act on our behalf in ways that move us forward in truth, which means uncovering lies. You are not responsible for how the family has to explain why you no longer attend family events. You get to live your truth when you refuse to participate with violators. It is not your fault if the church gets a bad reputation because you finally quit the choir to get away from a known violator that the church protects. You have a right to feel safe. Too bad if the teacher gets fired because you press charges ten years after the abuse. You have a right to justice. We do not need family, organizations or jobs that protect violators. We must move forward in our conviction to heal!

July 25

Every time we make a choice, we are also making non-choices. Sometimes the non-choices will have a greater effect than the choices. If you choose to live openly as a survivor, you are not choosing to protect your family anymore. Sometimes the world responds to our non-choices with more resistance than our choices. No matter, how the world chooses to respond is not within our control and is not our responsibility. Our responsibility is to make the choices that move us forward.

July 26

For many survivors, negative emotions will remain a part of life due to the structural brain changes that have occurred as a result of the childhood trauma. On hyper-alert, feelings of insignificance, latent depression, triggers of irritation, random sadness, etc., may remain issues for us. However, these issues do not have to prevent us from living fully if we go within and be the "watcher" of our inner space instead of reacting to these feeling whenever they arise. We can train the brain not to respond to the hyper-alert alarms. We can observe the alerts, but make decisions from a space of stillness.

July 27

The world can feel so cold for people who have been traumatized at any age and in any way. Our best defense is to raise above the world to reach a level of warmth. Everyone knows that heat rises. When you are operating at a lower level of functioning, the world is extremely cold. You may have difficulty with relationships, suffer from self-hate or remain in a constant state of negativity. You may keep trying to add layers to stay warm, such as settling for dysfunctional relationships or attaching to negative identities. However, the task is to rise to a higher level and take off the layers.

July 28

When critics ask why we focus on the past, we can respond, "so that it stops repeating itself." We can no longer be victims of childhood sexual abuse. More children are victimized each day. They too will remain silent. So we are their voice. We must keep talking until society understands that effects of child victimization do not go away because we get older. We are the voices of the children.

July 29

As human beings, we have a tendency to allow people in our lives who confirm our beliefs about the world. The problem for survivors is that as we heal our beliefs about the world change to a healthier perspective. That causes us to grow out of some relationships. Healing sometimes means creating new relationships to support the new you.

July 30

Separating from loved ones whom we seek love and affirmation from is extremely difficult. In theory, families provide a sense of belonging and unconditional love and support. In reality, families (or some members) tend to expect more from survivors than what is reasonable to give when they demand silence. Many survivors try to give it, for a short period or a long period, until they realize how much deeper it makes the pain. Then the concept of the family has to be redefined. There are many conditions that determine when we cut dysfunctional ties that we have with family members. Age, financial dependence, relationship to the violator, frequency of contact, our marital status, and our social support system may be considered. Deciding to cut ties can move you leaps and bounds in the healing process, but it can also leave you drowning in insecurity and regret if done too soon or without proper support.

July 31

Many survivors never learn how to have intimate sex, sex connected to emotional longing. Often we settle for partners who sexually interact with us the way the violator did. The sex centers on the partner's needs rather than our own. When we are not focusing on our partner's needs, we may become disinterested in sex. But we can transition into sex that focuses on our needs. Foreplay can take up to an hour just to get us in the mood. It might start with cuddling during a movie, a hot shower, a massage or playing a game of questions. Emotional intimacy should lead to sexual fulfillment if given enough time and attention. Healing our sexual selves is part of healing our emotional selves.

8: PANDORA'S BOX

Forgiveness of violators is not required for healing. Forgiveness is an experience that may or may not arise at some point on the healing journey for survivors. It is neither necessary nor sufficient for survivors to reclaim their lives and live an abundantly healthy life.

August 1

Incest and sexual abuse occur so freely because we cling to a system that supports the violation. It is impossible to heal fully and hold onto and continue to support the system that so freely enables violation. There is a reason why 90% of violators are men, even when victims are male. There is a reason that 80% of victims are female, even when the violator is a female. Sexual violation is not about sex but about power and dominance. People who violate are not seeking orgasm. They are seeking arousal through a feeling of power and dominance. Sex is the tool, a means to an end. Most violators are in sexual relationship already and no one needs to violate another person to have sex. There is plenty of sex available in this world. As survivors, we owe it to ourselves to understand, not from an emotional point, but from an academic point, what it means to live in a male-dominant world. We must understand the connection between male-dominance and rape culture and the silence in which we live. Male dominance goes far beyond equal employment and sexual harassment. It is an iceberg. It may be the voice of adult survivors that can shake its core, but only if we are willing to heal by any means necessary, only if we are willing to take on an academic challenge and a humanitarian purpose in our healing. Our personal victimization is a tiny part of a gigantic problem. When we understand the bigger issue, healing the personal issues become easier.

August 2

Learning to love yourself is about creating the evidence. You can reflect on the evidence at the end of the day, each month or from year to year. Think about how often you allow yourself to self-reflect without judgment. You know if you still struggle to look in the mirror and smile to affirm your commitment to self-love. You can do a heart check and know if you denied requests that did not feel right and responded when opportunities did. You know if you are still expecting someone else to take care of you. You collect the evidence from day-today. If you are collecting evidence of loving others more than you love yourself, then lean into the self-awareness so that the energy can change in your direction.

August 3

The way to change any relationship is to focus on the one person that you can change. That person is you. When you change your relationship with yourself, all other relationships that you have in the world will change. That is so much easier than working on relationships at work, home, church, school and in your social circles. When you trust yourself, affirm yourself and sit with yourself, then it is easier for people to be around you and for you to be around people. Ironically, the way to practice self-acceptance is in your relationships with others. But the focus must be on you rather than the relationship. Every time you see conflict arising you get to look within at your expectations of wanting someone to fulfill you because you have not learned to fulfill yourself. Then you get to practice fulfilling yourself. Meanwhile, you allow a lot of room for trial and adjustment.

August 4

Are you waiting for your mother to nurture you? Many survivors spend much of their adult lives trying to create the relationship they wished they had with their mothers. Survivors often want desperately to be nurtured as they resent their mother at the same time. Survivors often want their mothers to heal so that they can fit into the survivor's idea of mothering. Given your mother's own healing path, she did what she knew (or did not know) to do. If she knew better, she would have done better. You could not change her then, and you cannot change her now. No matter what dysfunction separated her from her truest loving self, healing is a path that must be chosen by the individual. No one can choose it for another. You have chosen your healing path. You must be ready to walk it without grasping and looking back for your mother's hand.

August 5

At the end of the day on what do you reflect? Do you reflect on your history, your present or your future? Reflect on the past and you may sleep on regret. Reflect on the future and you may sleep on anxiety. No matter what the day brings, when your head hits the pillow, let it lay in the peace of the present moment. Whatever happened, we survived. We did all that we could do and said all that needed to be heard that day. No need to try to live tomorrow in our head before it comes, or ruminate on the yesterday that we cannot fix. Do whatever you need to do to let peace wash over you each night. Read affirmations, watch a comedy (not the news), listen to a meditation or pray to relieve stress and offer a state of gratitude so that you can rest in peace each night, then awake with the promise of a new day.

August 6

Many survivors have felt love for their violator at some point, and now feel a lot of guilt and shame. Memories of our compliance make our stomach turn, our head hurt, and our soul ache. It brings up insurmountable guilt and shame, so we do not talk about it. We have lived with the assumption that we are the only survivor that loved and "cooperated" with the abuser. But that is not true. Many survivors felt or still feel love for the violator. We wanted to feel love when someone presented love-related behaviors to us as children. Since the mind seeks consistency, it readily accepted that the violator's grooming behaviors indicated love. A child certainly does not have the maturity to sort through the deceit and manipulation. We freely loved as a child victim, until the day of understanding arrived. Then we began to hate ourselves. The adult self showed up on the scene and processed the situation as if they were there the entire time. But we were child victims, doing what human beings are supposed to do freely... love.

August 7

Childhood sexual abuse comes with two deep layers. There is the physical contact, which may have been initiated by the violator with mental manipulation or the use of physical force, or a combination of the two. No matter what level of force was used, the second layer of sexual abuse is typically the same for most victims. The violator places the blame on the victim. The victim is made to believe that they are the one who caused the acts to occur. From "You're so beautiful that I have to have you" to "If you did not want it, it would not have happened." Survivors are sexually traumatized and then emotionally victimized by being forced to take the blame for making themselves a victim. The second layer of the abuse is often deeper than the first layer. It is the second layer that keeps survivors awake at night, hyper-alert during the day, feeling ashamed during intimacy, numbed out during festive times and confused during confrontations. Taking the blame for sexual abuse can negatively affect self-esteem, self-preservation, self-empowerment, self-fulfillment, and the general sense of self. The good news is that when you come to terms with your innocence, the innocence of your inner child, it causes an immediate shift into an empowering space of self-acceptance that can fast-forward healing. In case it has not sunk in yet; it was not your fault!

August 8

We cannot heal by imitation. The healing process is unique to us all in spite of all that we share in common. The betrayal may be similar, the pain familiar, the shame common and the fear mutual among us. But we vary in areas of strengths and weaknesses, resources and support, beliefs and awareness, situations and circumstances. No matter how much we admire any survivor, imitating what we see or what we think they do will not put us where they are on the path. We must go within to customize our path on a daily basis. We learn by our trials and errors. We grow more by reflecting on our patterns than by reflecting on others. Of course, we learn from others, but only to the degree that we understand ourselves. Trust that you are exactly where you are meant to be on the healing journey. You are not the same place on the journey as you were last year. You will not be here this time next year. But while you are here, embrace where you are and value the uniqueness of your journey.

August 9

Given the choice of feeling alone and rejected by doing what we know is right, or being accepted by agreeing with others that we know are wrong, research confirms that 50% of people would choose acceptance instead of doing what they know is right. Research also shows that people who feel rejected have depressed brain chemistry and are more vulnerable to suicidal thoughts. It is easy to understand why many survivors remain attached to their families, even when they protect the violators or offer no support for healing. It is also easy to understand why many survivors suffer from thoughts of suicide. But that also means that we must be vigilant in our efforts to create safe space for survivors so that they are never alone or have to feel rejected by the entire world. As we heal, we must light the path for others.

August 10

Mind-blindness is a term that describes a tendency to misunderstand or misinterpret other people's thoughts, feelings or actions. It is a common long-term effect of childhood trauma. Mind-blindness means that a person tends to assume that the person they interact with sees the world exactly as they do. Whatever is in the mind of the survivor, they assume is also in the other person's mind. Mind-blindness is the reason many survivors have difficulty in relationships. They struggle with the ability to detect deception and manipulation. Often, they are taken advantage of by other wounded people that they innocently invite into their lives. It is also difficult to express expectations to people who do genuinely care because people who have mind-blindness assume that people know exactly how to treat them. Mind-blindness is difficult to change because the person is unaware of their own mind's tendency to act on the world this way. Moving beyond mind-blindness usually only happens within a relationship where someone is patient enough with a survivor to reflect their tendency back to them in a loving way. If you have struggled all your life with all types of relationships, work, friends, and partners, then you may suffer from mind-blindness. Take some time to learn more about it. Once you become aware of your patterns, then it is much easier to change and heal your approach to relationships.

August 11

Practice self-soothing. The survivor's mind can go haywire easily and frequently. Negative thoughts, feeling of loneliness, anger or sadness can show up randomly. When these states of mind occur, it is good to know how to self-sooth. There are many activities that can calm the mind. Music is a great start. It is good to have a tune on your mobile phone or mp3 player just for these occasions. Make sure it is a tune that lifts you up, not take you further under. Exercise is a bigger commitment but brings bigger results in the long run. The best exercise is the exercise that you will do, but it cannot rely on another person. For example, you cannot reliably self-soothe with exercise if you will only exercise with a partner. Running, swimming and biking are easy to do alone, so they are better soothing exercises than tennis or team sports. Try watching stand-up comedy on television. They are easy to find on demand if you have a television subscription. You can also find plenty of comedy online if you have access to a computer. Write an email to a friend. Talk about good news. Do not make mention of how you are feeling or why you are writing the email. Just create positive interaction. Take a quick nap to recharge. Sometimes bad moods are our body's way of telling us to rest. When you feel these moods, just remember to practice the task of "self-soothing." It takes a lot of trial and error. So keep practicing until it becomes a way of being and your general state of mind is a sense of peace.

August 12

If only our childhood trauma would excuse us from adult trauma. If only we did not have loved ones die too young, lose good jobs, fall sick to serious illness, have children with troubled minds, get divorced, or fall victim to natural disasters. Life does not give you a resting period to deal with your childhood trauma. There is no period where you are assured not to have any more trauma added to your plate until you have healed. We have to continue to be in the world, to survive in the world even as we take on the challenges and additional traumas of adulthood. No, it does not seem fair. There is no magic moment where life just works itself out. So we might as well let go of the idea of waiting. Healing has to be active, consistent and persistent. We sometimes have to do double duty and address issues of trauma from the past and present life challenges together to secure our brighter future. However, the more we heal from the past, the more effectively we deal with challenges that arise in the present.

August 13

Females have been the target of sexual violence in the world for a long, long time. When we consider the history of rape, forced marriages, and the sex trade, there is a good chance that most of us had mothers who were survivors themselves and lived in silence all their lives. That does not let them off the hook for not being better at caring for us. However, it may offer you permission to stop wishing that your mother had done more for you. Not all victims become survivors, but you can.

August 14

Childhood sexual abuse leaves deep wounds. The truth is that most adults have some wounds that they have not addressed. Unfortunately, survivors have a tendency to attract others with deep wounds into our space. There is a certain level of comfort we feel with wounded people because it is easy to recognize their pain. Often we end up surprised that these people end up hurting us even though they know about our trauma. We expect people who know our history of abuse to respond to us based on what they know about our past. However, people will only respond to us based on their past, no matter how much they know about our past. The conflict causes the clashing of pain rather than healing.

August 15

We have all asked the question, "why." But there is no response that will take away our grief not matter how we ask the question. Go ahead and grieve. And when you are done grieving a new question will emerge. "What do I do with the pain I have been given?" This question can lead to transformation. Learning how to make lemonade from life's lemons is a survivor's specialty when we are on the healing path. We remember that to drink from a glass that is half-full, we have to tilt the glass or drink from a straw. But even a half-full glass of lemonade can quench your thirst.

August 16

Not every case of "childhood" sexual abuse and incest ends in childhood. There are cases of sexual abuse that never end, not even in adulthood. Some violators taunt their victims far into adulthood. Fathers continue to intimately touch their adult daughters. Aunts continue to make sexual comments about the nephew's body. Brothers continue to walk into the bathroom while sisters shower. The pastor continues a clandestine relationship with the church member that was his child victim. The former babysitter continues to touch the grown man's genitals just like she did when he was a boy whenever she attends the summer cookout. The sister's husband still fondles the sister he raped when she was a child. Meanwhile, the adult victims continue to hide their fear and smile as if they are fine, or have to constantly fight to protect themselves while the silence remains. Healing is for everyone. No one has to suffer from this crime all of their lives. There is room on the healing path for you. Know that you are not walking alone.

August 17

A key to healing is "loyalty to oneself." We often practice loyalty to others, but fail to extend ourselves the same loyalty. No matter what your history has been, love you and forgive you. Give yourself a thousand more chances. You deserve it. You have no reason to fear. There is nothing to prove. There is no one that you have to put first. You are the center of your universe. So that you do not need to be the center of anyone else's.

August 18

Going within is like going in the caves to find the treasure. If you only look right near the surface, you will not find the most valuable treasures. You have to go into the cave of your mind and get sweaty and dirty and stinky as you get deeper and deeper. It may get darker and darker and more difficult to breathe. But you have to go in far enough if you want to get to the treasure of peace. You have to dig deep to find the beauty of you because what you think the violator took from you, is not possible to be taken. It just got buried.

August 19

We should not look at the victim's response to trauma to determine who is at fault. The law is clear. A child cannot offer consent to an adult. Theories of child development are clear. Children require trusting relationships with adults that do not compromise their physical, emotional, or social well-being. Still, the brain plays many tricks on the mind just to survive, including believing that you made the abuse happen. The violator was in control the entire time of the abuse and is still in control as long as you blame yourself for the abuse. As long as you are willing to hold onto the secret, you maintain an intimate bond with the violator. Blaming yourself also maintains the bond. The more we blame ourselves, the more room we give violators to do what they do. Give yourself space to be angry, sad, resentful, etc., as long as you break the bond. It may even take a while to release the shame. But the blame has got to stop now. It is too big of an obstacle to healing.

August 20

The next time a person says that you need to "move on," remind them that that is exactly what you did when you were a child, and this is where it got you. It is bad enough that the court system has a statute of limitation on childhood sexual abuse charges. Society denies us the right to heal as well. When the violator finishes unraveling our childhood we are not allowed to go crying to adults once we become one. When the abuse ends, if the abuse ends, victims spend what is left of their childhood sucking up the pain and tucking it away to prepare for an adult life of pretending of they do not hurt. This denial is unreasonable and prevents healing. Survivors of childhood sexual abuse and incest need to heal, not move on.

August 21

If you do not love yourself then giving or receiving love to or from anyone else is not possible. Love is more about who we are than what we choose. When we allow ourselves to be an expression of love from within, then that love will be reflected back to us. But trying to create love from the outside is clinging and grasping at a mirage. Today is a great day to invest in loving yourself so that the love can be reflected back to you in all of your relationships. Replacing the statement that you do not love yourself with the statement that you are learning to love yourself is a great way to start. Count to three and say, "I am learning to love myself."

August 22

Some survivors feel as if they have some work to do on forgiveness of self, and other survivors clearly believe that there is nothing to forgive. Both are right. Every survivor gets to determine what issues are essential to them. Whatever we did to survive got us this far. Many of us took on dysfunctional patterns to survive, whether that was acquiring an addiction, looking for an escape or using perfectionism to indulge our denial. Forgiving ourselves for our ways of coping can help us look within and take responsibility for our lives. It can also be a way to invite the inner child to have a front row seat in our lives so that she/he can heal. The simple words "I'm sorry" repeated to your inner child may do wonders. When survivors recognize a need for self-forgiveness on the path, it is not because we are taking responsibility for the abuse or taking blame away from the violator. It is a way to reconcile with ourselves. It is a way to give ourselves what we may have sought from others.

August 23

Cycles are patterns of events or behaviors that repeat themselves. Cycles can strengthen us, or weaken us, depending on the pattern. But, a cycle always strengthens itself. Each time a cycle is repeated, it is strengthened. It becomes easier and easier to repeat. You are just the host of the cycle. Unfortunately, many survivors get stuck in dysfunctional cycles. For example, there is the trigger, fear, attack, and the trigger, fear, withdraw cycles. There is the cycle of attention and relinquishment of power, where whenever someone gives you attention, you relinquish all power to them. The love to hate cycle is where every love relationship ends in hate. Much of our pain is connected to the cycles that we keep alive in our lives. It can be difficult to see the strongest cycles in our lives because they have a life of their own as a result of so much strengthening. But if you keep getting the same results in your life that means that you are in a cycle. You can only break out of a cycle by becoming the observer of your mind and behavior. But all cycles can be broken.

August 24

Commitment to heal is a leap of faith because healing does not take away any pain in the beginning. Healing brings up the pain and compels you to deal with it. Commitment to heal does not allow you to forget the pain or ignore the pain. Healing requires that you turn the pain inside-out. Each tear that falls washes away the shame. Each heartache brings you closer to the truth about your family environment. Your desire to isolate distances you from the lies that you once accepted as truth. Do not worry so much about the pain that comes with healing. It is all part of the process. Trust the process.

August 25

The brain needs much attention and care to repair itself. In the absence of adequate information, the brain is likely to use you to remain a victim, rather than you using your brain to heal. The unchallenged brain will remain static with fear that produces compulsive negative thinking as well as dysfunctional patterns of behavior. The information you should know about your brain includes the effects of medication on depression, natural ways to improve your thinking and mood, the best food choices for the brain and the effect of childhood trauma on the brain. The internet allows access to all these topics on video, in research articles, and on websites. Use your mind to inform your brain so that the brain does not continue to repeat the outdated messages and patterns of behavior. Knowledge is power, and the most powerful exchange of knowledge is between the mind and the brain.

August 26

The most difficult task to work on for healing is to end the seeking happiness outside of oneself. Society embeds this dysfunctional behavior in all of us, survivor or not. But breaking the cycle is likely more difficult for survivors because of our trauma issues. There are many ways that we seek happiness outside of ourselves. One is by expecting a particular response from someone. Remember, we do not get to choose how people respond to us in life. Loving someone does not require them to love us in return. It certainly does not require them to love us in the exact way that we interpret love in our heads. Another way we seek happiness outside of ourselves is by disclosing the abuse. We wrongly assume that when people know about our experience of sexual abuse that somehow a relationship will change. But it usually does not. If a person was not in sync with you enough to create a fulfilling relationship, then disclosing the abuse will not improve the relationship. Another way we seek happiness is through our identities, such as parent, partner or career person. We work so hard at maintaining our identities that we feel intense pain whenever our identities are threatened. Dare to go within to create happiness without attachments, expectations, demands and seeking from another person.

August 27

Healing is a natural process that happens when we get out of our own way. Many people think they have been trying to heal, but what they have been doing is trying to get out of pain as quickly as they can. Healing involves a willingness to sit with the pain, not in complacency, but to build the tools to move forward. Healing is as natural as a tree growing toward the sky. It is as natural as your hair growing back each time you cut it. It is as natural a child learning to talk and the baby bird learning how to fly. This does not mean healing is painless. It is simply natural.

August 28

Turning our attention away from violators, dysfunctional family members and unsupportive people are an important part of the healing journey. They eat up too much energy to focus on them, much less try to change them. You cannot change them and yourself too. You cannot depend on them to change so that it will be easier for you to change either. Often, healing requires us to circumvent these people. We have to decide the healthiest place to fit them into our lives, even if that means keeping them out of our lives so that we can focus on ourselves.

August 29

Life is forgiving in that single decisions do not usually end in severe consequences (although sometimes they do). However, it is the patterned decisions that form our lives. Once our thoughts, actions, and desires turn into patterns, then our lives are at the mercy of those patterns. The worst part is that patterns become invisible to our minds. They are difficult for us to recognize even when they bring consequences that deepen our scars. Healing opens us up to the patterns that dictate our lives. That includes patterns surrounding our sexuality. Many survivors develop dysfunctional patterns of expressing or suppressing sexuality. They may attempt to hide their sexuality with excess weight or poor grooming. They may solicit affirmation through sex. They may remain in victim mode within their sexual relationships by denying themselves sexual pleasure while accepting responsibility for the sexual pleasure of a partner. Survivors sometimes refuse to look at or touch their body. All of these patterns form a dysfunctional sexual experience that may influence our nonsexual experiences as well. Disconnecting from our sexual selves does not make us safer in the world. When we disconnect at this basic level of existence behind closed doors, then what we do in the world may reflect that disconnection. Healing our sexual selves is often an important part of healing that gets ignored. But you do not get to pass on this responsibility. Healing our sexual selves prepare us to make direct demands in the world and toward an individual, unapologetically.

August 30

Most survivors rely heavily on defense mechanisms to survive. Defense mechanisms are psychological responses to threats. They are distortions of reality that arrive through the unconscious mind to give us hope and make us believe that we are worth being in the world and being loved and that we are safe. Survivors are usually overly attached to defense mechanisms, which may block us from moving from surviving to thriving in our lives. The most common defenses are denial, repression, projection and reaction formation. These all distort the reality of our perceptions. Healing gives us more accurate perceptions of our world.

August 31

Trauma does not make you stronger. It makes you weak, fearful and psychologically disoriented. People living in pain make worse decisions because choices are typically reactionary. Just because you are still alive does not mean you are living, and it certainly does not mean that you are strong. The adage, "What does not kill you makes you stronger" is a myth. What does make a survivor stronger is exerting a will to live, not just stay alive. The exertion of will makes you stronger because you commit to healing, even when you do not know what direction to take on the path. You take on a responsibility for learning, stretching, growing and moving in a positive direction. Do not settle for just being alive after the trauma. Become stronger, and stronger and stronger, through a commitment to healing.

9: GUINEA PIG LEARNS TO SPEAK

Most people are more afraid of our pain than we are. They fail to realize that we have carried this junk inside of us for so long that we have learned how to live with it already. When we disclose, the pain is not new, only the visibility of it is new.

September 1

You did not come in the world to live from a position of fear. The fear instinct is to keep us alive. It is a response. When the fear response is triggered our bodies transform automatically. Our pupils dilate, heart beats faster, breathing increases, blood flows faster, and hormones are released that help us ignore pain and run faster or fight harder. We have a completely separate nervous system to help us respond to threats. It is called the sympathetic nervous system and is a short-term response system to gets us to safety. We have gotten used to living with the sympathetic nervous system in overdrive because we were never out of danger. That is why we often have health issues, as well as relationship issues. We usually have to retrain our bodies as well as our mind on the healing path. We can learn how to breathe for tranquility, exercise to slow down our brain and heart and eat to balance our hormones. Healing has to pay attention to all of these systems as well.

September 2

"Perspective-taking" is a skill that begins to develop in childhood and is critical to social competence. When we have good skills in this area, we can read body language and understand intonations and voice inflections that tweak the meaning of the spoken words. This skill helps us to predict, with a fair amount of accuracy, whether someone is genuinely interested in us or if we should be suspicious of a person. It also helps us to sustain relationships with reciprocity instead of giving too much or taking too much. Unfortunately, this critical skill is often lacking in adult survivors of childhood sexual abuse because this skill needs a particular environment to fully develop. That environment must offer consistency, predictability, and safety. A developing child must have safe space to make mistakes and be offered positive feedback for guidance. These ingredients are often absent in a home where childhood sexual abuse and incest occur. This lack of healthy guidance is a major reason many survivors have social skills that do not yield them the social experiences they desire. The solution is to notice every reaction, every response that you have. You must question yourself regularly. Is there a different way that another person can see this situation? What would make someone respond to me in a way that hurt me? What did I not see? What am I not understanding? How did I get in my own way? As we learn to perspective-take, we become less rigid and more open. When our lives become more open, then it will be easier for the right people to enter.

September 3

Memories sometimes break through, and when they do, they are breaking through for a reason. Recovering lost memories is part of the healing process that includes recovering lost pain. Memories come up to be healed when you are strong enough. Memories are not there to harm you but to heal you. You have to allow the memory to exist to know what needs to be healed. Coded messages within recovered memories include: 1) The abuse was worse than you think. Your journey has only just begun. 2) Someone who you thought was safe all these years was not looking out for your good. You have to find a way to have peace with that person based on the reality of your past rather than the lie you have been living all these years. 3) You have overlooked your resilience. See what tools your little child used to escape that you have abandoned as you aged. The memories are calling your attention to return to the tools. 4) There is an explanation for the "odd" behavior that people keep complaining about in your life. The memories are offering insight. Memories cannot hurt you, no matter how scary they are. Whatever the memory reveals, you have already survived. Now it is time to heal.

September 4

Although survivors may have developed dysfunctional patterns to survive, we should not make the assumption that all of our survival patterns are dysfunctional. Sometimes we disconnect from our inner child because we only associate negative behaviors with the inner child and ignore the specialties of the inner child. As memories return to you, and your inner child reveals the experiences that you are now ready to heal, look for the good in the child as well. Maybe there was academic brilliance that allowed the child to escape reality, or artistic brilliance that the child used as a distraction. The child may have been great at making friends so that she/he could have a haven. The child might have been disciplined, task-oriented, self-motivated or mature so that success came easily. You may have turned away from these traits and tools as you turned your back on your inner child. Despite what your adult self is willing to believe, the child who experienced the abuse did not give up. The child was an active participant in the plan for survival. So, though there is plenty to learn and unlearn, some of the tools you need to move you forward may already be present within you.

September 5

Too often when survivors of childhood sexual abuse disclose for the first time, there is an expectation of "a story." You do not owe anyone a story. What we choose to share is our experience of sexual abuse. Stories are meant to be shared and enjoyed with the world for the purpose of creating interest, amusement or entertainment. However, disclosing our experience of childhood sexual abuse should not be minimized to such a context. Survivors, in search of empathy, sometimes offer details about abuse in exchange for the compassion they hope to receive. Disclosing that you are a survivor of childhood sexual abuse is enough. You do not have to risk unpleasant feelings of uncertainty from telling people information in the hope of affirmation. We give up too much personal power by offering deeply personal information about ourselves in the hope of receiving affirmation. If we preserve our boundaries, including details of the abuse, for occasions that they are most relevant to sharing, instead of seeking, then we are less likely to be disappointed. You do not owe anyone a story.

September 6

You need people to support you on your journey. But there is not any particular person that you need. Expecting family members to be our main support is often a recipe for setbacks and family conflict. You have to figure out a plan to heal within the family structure that you were faced with before you started to heal. As you heal, your family dynamics will automatically change. But that does not mean that it will change the way that you want. It could reveal to you the beauty that you could not see while you were so deep in denial, or it could show you the deep dysfunction that supported your denial. Whatever healing reveals to you is for you to understand and respond to, not necessarily your family members.

September 7

When you have mind-blindness you may fall in love easily, and you assume the person loves you the same way. You may make sacrifices for people because you assume they need you. You may take on a lot of responsibility because you believe the world needs your input to keep working. That is because whatever you think or feel is what you believe other people think and feel. Therefore, you may not spend much time trying to understand those around you. You more likely invest your time in trying to get those around you to behave based on your understanding of the world. Even this explanation may be difficult to understand if you are stuck. But that is ok too because you will not always be stuck. You just have not yet had the combination of experiences the move you from that space. Rely on people that you trust to give you feedback about your interpretations of the world.

September 8

If your focus in the world is what people need to do differently or how the world is not responding to your needs, you may have mind-blindness. Mind-blindness is the failure to view the world from other people's view. It creates conflict in relationships and often isolates survivors from the world. You can only see the world based on your interest. The way out of this trap is to pay attention to the assumptions you make about the world and other people during your everyday interactions.

September 9

It is easier to complain for years to a person for them to treat you better than it is to walk away from a person who does not value you. It is easier to rant and rave about the people who walk into your life because you have no selection process in place than it is to make conscious choices about the people you invite into your life. Too often we grow accustomed to asking others to love us in ways that we do not yet love ourselves. We ask others to make room for us when we have not made any room for ourselves. When we consciously make rules and decisions that help us lovingly govern and direct our lives, then we will not spend our time hoping for others to change so that we can be happy. Only those who have patterns of behavior that are consistent with our life rules will qualify to be in our lives in the first place. Keep in mind that these are not the same dysfunctional rules that keep us in a box. These are healthy rules that make it safe for us to come out of our box and know that we will survive.

September 10

Learning to express feelings with a range of emotions is important to mental health. How many emotions can you think of in the next 10 seconds? For some survivors, anger, sadness, fear and happy are the only emotions they feel. Using more words may get you closer to the internal processes to work through whatever is coming up to be healed. Practice expressing your feelings without using sentiments of angry, afraid, happy and sad (no synonyms allowed) for a day, week or month. If sad is the first emotion that you feel, then ask yourself, "why am I sad"? Keep asking why until relevant information is revealed. You may be feeling abandoned. Perhaps you are frustrated by a feeling of inadequacy. You can explore what "happy" means too. Maybe you feel noticed, accepted, affirmed, validated, protected or significant. Try to write down a list of feelings so that you can choose one that is most accurate. The more ways you use to go within, the more accurate and appropriate your responses to the world are likely to be

September 11

The average survivor is victimized by three violators before the age of eighteen. The child victim likely lived in a dysfunctional environment that led to a compromised sense of self and misperceptions about the world. The first violator puts the victim further at risk for delayed social development by creating a horrifying experience that the child's undeveloped brain cannot adequately process. Once a child is violated and living in a dysfunctional environment, it is likely that they will not learn how to protect personal boundaries. They may not be able to properly read cues of danger. They may have an unhealthy and harmful respect for authority or family, and a freeze brain response to unwanted interactions. Victimization can breed victimization because abuse compromises development.

September 12

Survivors need listeners, and they are hard to find. Loved ones tend to be the worst listeners because they want to make us feel better. Instead of listening, they try to fix us. But only we can fix ourselves. When we talk we are trying to sort through all of the crazy in our head, the self-hate, the fear, the guilt, the shame, the blame, the rage, the will to die and the feeling of not being enough. But we cannot lay it out neatly packaged because we unravel it only through conversation. Statements that tell us that you believe our truth are most helpful. You believe that how we feel is a valid response. You believe that what we say happened did happen. You believe that we can heal. You believe that we are completely innocent in what happened to us. Instead of trying to fix, supporters should just try to hear and affirm. Trust us to heal if safe space to mourn the loss of childhood is established.

September 13

Healing is a lifelong journey. There is no cure for what we have. However, we can have peace, without resistance if we stay on the healing path. We can learn to live without constant conflict with life, self and others. We can learn to enjoy living. We can live without depression. We can have successful long-term relationships. Despite our past, we can live with gratitude. Healing is active; it is never done. But there are all sorts of goodies that come from the art and practice of healing.

September 14

Hiding anger is not the same as healing anger. Many survivors learn how to hide their anger, or, at least, we think we are hiding it. We move about life without any healthy outlet to acknowledge what happened to us as children. There is sometimes a struggle in our sexual relationships because we refuse to acknowledge and work through anger about the abuse. We may become angry with our partners instead of expressing anger toward the violator. Sometimes we struggle in our relationships with our children because we demand that they show the strength of an adult. We may display anger toward them for acting like children instead of allowing ourselves to be present with the anger about our childhood. We may take any opportunity to lash out at another person to release the unacknowledged anger that resides within us. These are just a few ways that we may hide our anger while we insist that we do not feel anger about the abuse. These patterns are a part of our denial that allows us to believe that we were not affected by the abuse. Unfortunately, it puts us further from the truth, and further behind on the healing path. If we pay attention to our thoughts and feelings about the abuse, we can get to the truth faster.

September 15

Healing is a lot of "stuff," stuff we have to uncover just to start the journey. We have to uncover our denial; we have to uncover the trauma, uncover the effects sexual abuse has had on our lives. We have to learn how to live. We have to teach people how to treat us differently as we learn how to live. There is too much to do to think that healing is an event that just happens, or that we can take care of all at once. Think about all of the activities that you have to do just to prepare for one ordinary day. You have to set your alarm, get out of bed when it goes off, leave yourself just the right amount of time to take care of all of your grooming needs, eat breakfast, get to work or school and get more nutrients in your system so you can last the rest of the day. You cannot do all of those tasks at the same time. They have to be organized, and the way that people organize them depends on their lifestyle and experience and life goals. No one told you exactly how to prepare for work each day. You just learned it by being involved in living. You paid attention, kept up with expectations, had some goals and looked for ways to be comfortable as you carried out routine. Healing works the same way. This book reminds you what it could look like and throw out some pointers as you find your way. Trust that you are finding your way with each pointer.

September 16

Many survivors of childhood sexual abuse hold onto guilt because they were the victim of more than one violator. Society tells us that if the same experience happens more than once, then it must be our fault. We apply that reasoning to our experience of abuse and manifests it as guilt and shame. Well, what society does not tell us is that 50% of survivors are victimized by more than one violator. The average number of violators is three. We must look at the environment that silences victims and the patterns of the violators to make sense of the revictimization, not blame ourselves.

September 17

Healing is contagious. So, find positive people who understand the healing path to travel the journey. They do not have to be perfect, just positive. Spend time with people who are creative, live with acceptance, and embrace gratitude as a way of life. Find the people who thirst for life and drink at the well of wellness. As you practice living this way, you will meet these like-minded people. When you find them, build a healthy relationship with them. They may come as disguised to you. Therefore, you must pay attention. They may not be the same race, same age group, same religion, same status or same sexual orientation as you. It is the kindred spirit that you need, so those demographic characteristics will not matter. But try not to cling to these people, for that defeats the purpose. As you heal, the right people will flow into and out of your life, always leaving you further on the path and carrying less baggage.

September 18

No one has to teach a child how to love themselves. Human beings are prewired to love themselves. "Not Loving Oneself" is what has to be taught. Adult survivors were taught to not love themselves. Learning self-love as an adult is like trying to learn a foreign language as we age. It is doable but much more difficult than when we were young. We have to immerse ourselves in the language of self-love to become proficient. Spend time in environments that speak the language of love. Read books, watch television, socialize around the experience of love. Avoid environments that encourage your primary language of conflict, criticism, doubt and confusion. That is the language of "other". We want to master the language and life of self, "self-love".

September 19

A healing heart expresses love as a primary tool, love without the attachment demands. The healing mind expresses self-discipline as the primary tool, the discipline without the self-criticism. The healing soul expresses peace as the primary tool, peace without detachment. Healing offers us the functional tools to live in the present moment without the reaction drama. Fewer and fewer responses come from fear and pain, even though we may continue to feel fear and pain. We can feel negative emotions without responding to them because now emotions play a more appropriate role in our lives. Instead of being the director of our lives, emotions point us toward insight. The insight leads us back to love, discipline, and peace.

September 20

Using "I" language can help us look within. Mind-blindness usually keeps the conversation on the other person. If we can remember to start our assessments of the world with "I" instead of he, she or they, then we can work our way out of mind-blindness. Mind-blindness, after all, is just a patterned practice. It is not permanent. We can change it. In fact, once we start working on it, we may see some significant changes soon.

September 21

Many survivors take on responsibility for the abuse because of their eventual response to the violator. Often, we play over in our heads a point where we did not stop the abuse from happening. There is often a pivotal point when we gave up. We gave up or gave in because the reality dawned on us that we were in a hopeless situation. Like in the movie, the reality set in that we were going to be taken by the bad guys. This reality often sets in after grooming has taken place. The violation might be physically forceful, verbally deceitful, nonverbally gestured. Either way, our brain sent the message that told us the best option for survival was to no longer resist. Many of us know that exact moment and have played it over and over with the theme of guilt and shame in our head. That moment has fueled much of our negative thoughts. It interferes with healing because we never accepted that we were victims. We believe we had other options. This misperception is where the adult self, in an attempt to make sense of the world, often separates from the inner child who knows that there was no option.

September 22

The mother-child relationship is the most honored relationship of all. So, how do we reconcile the choice we make to be distant and to live in a truth that confronts the most precious relationship of all? Love is supposed to be unconditional, yet the price we pay for love is silence. Instead of being protected, we become the protectors. We protect the family secrets to uphold the wholesome reputation. Many survivors do choose to take the path of no resistance to maintain the precious mother-child bond, especially when mother behaves perfectly in every other way. But you have to choose the path that is right for you. Not even the mother-child relationship is more important than healing when you heal by any means necessary. This is not about having a love-hate relationship with your mother. It is about having a loving relationship with yourself.

September 23

Many survivors become physically obese as an unconscious means to protect themselves, feeling like their attractiveness invites danger (perhaps told that by some violators). First, beauty is not a vulnerability in the world. It is an advantage. Second, attractiveness is not directly related to size. Third, being overweight never protected anyone from a violator. Fourth, in reality, perpetrators are not "attracted" to vulnerability. They create it! Children are targeted because it is easier to create vulnerability in them since they are not cognitively developed enough to resist. So let go of the myth and give yourself permission to be your most beautiful and healthy self.

September 24

Some of the most serious people about healing are also the most serious about fitness. They are often at their workout stations by 5:00 am. If you schedule your workouts at this time, you will not have to worry about interruptions. No one else is going to call a meeting at 5:00 am. Our bodies also burn more calories when we workout at this time. The brain gets endorphin going, and we can think more clearly during the day as well. Getting up at this hour can also help us sleep better at night. Healing makes life easier, but healing is not easy. We must try new behavior to experience new feelings like real joy and peace and contentment. Early morning workouts could be the new behavior to try.

September 25

There are questions to ask ourselves when we feel disappointment, frustration and discontent. Questions that lead us within can return us to a state of power through personal responsibility. Who did I make responsible for my joy? How did I make this person responsible for my happiness? Did I turn my wants into needs? What did I not say or do because I was too afraid? These are just a few questions to ask when we find ourselves disappointed by situations. These types of questions keep the focus on you so that you can get the lesson. When we get the lesson we are no longer bitter, closed or angry about the situation. Lessons allow us to understand ourselves and others so that we can live more openly and authentically and draw similar people into our lives.

September 26

Excessive weight never makes a person unlovable. It is not a reason to beat up on yourself. Practicing self-love is important based on exactly the person you are right now. People who maintain a high standard of health do not focus on their weight. We focus on good living, and the weight tends to take care of itself. Most people know that they should eat well and exercise. The issue is one of motivation rather than knowledge. You can find someone to help motivate you. You may find a workout partner at your job or school. There are plenty of people in the same position of wanting to lose weight, but they lack motivation. Meanwhile, just love yourself the way you are and appreciate the change as it comes.

September 27

When you look in the mirror, you should see your beauty within and your resilience. Hopefully, you do not see yourself through the abuser's eyes. If you see yourself as weak and undeserving of real love, or ugly and unlovable, then you are in a place where you still identify with the abusers. You have separated from your truest self instead of separating from the abuser. Your self-judgment keeps you and the experience of abuse and the abuser intimately connected through the mind. Let go of the vision that the violator imposed on you and see yourself clearly.

September 28

The more complex our world becomes, the more distracted we are from what is inside. Most people do not spend time introspecting. Trauma is motivation to keep your guard up. Introspection remains a distant goal although it is necessary for healing. We have to go within to heal. That is where the trauma has been created. Confusion, distortion, and defensiveness all happen on the inside. We have to introspect, gently and lovingly with ourselves. We look inside to guide, not become self-critical. We look inside to understand, not to judge. We look inside to repair, not to focus on the broken. Like a car, you cannot just go through the car wash to keep your car running. You have to look under the hood when you hear it making noise, or if it fails to start, or if the ride is too bumpy. Unlike a car, though, there is no trade-in for the mind. You have to repair what you have.

September 29

You must go out of your mind to heal. Healing feels crazy at times because you have to go out of your mind to undo the dysfunctional patterns of being in the world. Only a person out of their mind willingly separates from the people called "family."

Only a person out of their mind willing reveals secrets that were never meant to be told and risk humiliation and rejection. Only a person out of their mind will choose their path, the healing path, where they let go of whatever does not serve them. Only a person out of their mind will commit to choosing painful truth over the familiar pain to move forward. Once you are out of you mind you relearn how to navigate through life.

September 30

Think about learning to read. Language is a natural process. Someone teaches you the sound of every letter. If you are lucky someone sits and listens to you read for a while when you are learning the basics. Then the rest is up to you. How much you practice and what level of books you read will determine how proficient you become. Typically, children will try to read all the words they see when they are learning how to read. They read advertisements, directions on a packet to magazines and road signs in addition to the standard books of the bedtime ritual. Literacy is critical to living independently. The ability to read is the ability to learn. The ability to learn is the key to knowledge. Children know that knowledge is power. The same is true for healing. Someone teaches us the basics of healing, like stay present, go within, and trust the process. We discuss these basics rituals in a variety of ways. But each person determines their investment in the practice of healing. The more a person is invested in the process, the more opportunities they look for to practice. You heighten your sense of awareness so you can process your experiences, just as a child sounds out words. You read, listen and involve yourself in as much matter related to healing as you can stand to develop your proficiency. Healing, like reading, is critical to living independently.

10: THE DAY AFTER TOMORROW

Healing should be holistic, and quality is far more important than quantity when it comes to healing resources. Quality resources on spiritual development, quality health, and life management are important as well as resources for adult survivors of childhood sexual abuse.

OCTOBER 1

There is plenty of "blame" to go around when processing our past. When a child is sexually abused, something has gone terribly wrong, and the child is the only innocent party. Until what went wrong is rectified, the person who was wronged is not responsible for the outcome of their situation. If you steal my identity and use up all of my financial resources, I will not be able to pay bills the next month. And what I need is for my debt collectors to have compassion. I need the legal system to help me seek justice. I need my friends and family to support me while I get back on my feet. Survivors of childhood sexual abuse are in need of this level of compassion and support. The person who betrayed us is the one who is responsible for the pain we have endured. The law falls short in helping us seek justice. Our family victimizes us over again by ignoring the effects of the trauma. It is as if they collectively put a knife in a child's back six inches and pulled it out only three inches so the child could stay alive. Then when we become adults, with the knife is still stuck three inches in our back, while we are told to stop crying. They assert that the knife has been there so long we should have gotten used to the pain by now. They are the heartless ones. They are the cowards. They stand by and judge while we spend our lives learning emotional yoga to try to reach the knife still stuck in our backs.

October 2

Our bodies did not betray us. Our bodies 'saved' us. Especially with ongoing molestation, the body adapts to its environment to survive. The body may stop fighting the abuse to survive, or the body may respond to the abuse by reciprocating desire. A response of cooperation (not consent because a child cannot offer consent) may be a necessity when a child cannot stop the abuse because the body knows that prolonged fighting will likely end in their demise. Just like POWs do whatever is necessary to survive, so do victims of childhood sexual abuse. Unfortunately, our misunderstanding of this causes us to reject our adult bodies instead of nurture it with love. Healing helps us to restore our body and mind.

October 3

Relationships are the garden of our emotional landscape in some ways. We should practice having a green thumb. Are you growing annuals or perennials? Annuals can bring much beauty, but they only last for a short season. You have to replant them every year, which is a lot of work. Perennials sustain themselves and provide beauty year after year. Even still, you have to do a lot of weeding in any garden. Weeds pop out of nowhere and can take over if left unattended. You have to continually pull the weeds and tend to the flowers. Survivors typically have a lot to learn about keeping healthy relationships. But if you think of them as a well-manicured garden you may get some clues about the "how to" have good ones.

October 4

Most violators do not retire. They remain filthy, arrogant, and shameless, because they can. There is little motivation for change given the support that violators typically receive. They are supported by victims who remain silent, family members who want to protect their reputation, and a culture that makes jokes about child molestation. So it is unlikely that you were the first victim or that you were the last victim of the criminal who violated you. Violators are not kind people who just happen to have part of a bad history. Violators are bad people who often present themselves as kind to cover up their evil. Child sexual offenders do not accidentally violate children. They typically plan it through well thought-out manipulation. They live with patterns and schemes to exploit the innocence of children and the fear of adults who will protect them. The world must stop cooperating, stop protecting and stop excusing these perpetrators.

October 5

Therapy is a common suggestion when we tell people about our experience. People are uncomfortable with what we tell them, so they recommend that we talk to someone who understands. Just because someone suggests therapy, does not mean that you should go, or that you need to go right away. There are healthy survivors who heal without professional intervention. There are also so many different types of therapy that a person who recommends a therapist is not necessarily offering good advice. Therapy can also do harm when it is used primarily to help survivors keep their secret. There are important reasons to seek therapy but therapy does not take away the need for listeners in our lives.

October 6

We do not have to settle for external success without internal peace. College degrees do not educate us about the effects of childhood sexual abuse. Physical fitness does not make you comfortable with your sex life. Making a lot of money will not make triggers go away. Working your way to the top will not stop the constant conflict in your life. Your fancy house will not hide your addiction forever. Insanity is not the most frequent side effect of childhood sexual abuse. Trying to hide the fact that you are a survivor is the most frequent side effect of childhood sexual abuse. The continuation of living patterns of victimization in spite of apparent success is a common side effect of sexual abuse. The refusal to lean into the healing journey because you are trying to "look healed", instead of healing, is the biggest side effect. So, are you really ready to heal?

October 7

Sexual abuse did not destroy our potential. Victimization may have interfered with our motivation, our discipline, and our vision, but it did not destroy our potential. Once we find the healing path, we will eventually be reintroduced us to our full potential. Childhood sexual abuse is traumatic, but, its effect is limited. Abuse has the greatest effect on our minds as it distorts our reality. It often distorts our reality about our potential. Living as a victim hides our power. The healing path restores our perception so that we can learn to live according to our true power and potential.

October 8

Many survivors isolate, hide, withdraw or detach because they see their experience of abuse as shameful, dirty, or disgraceful. However, it is not shameful to be a victim. It is shameful to be a violator. Is not dirty to be naïve as a child. It is dirty to for an adult to take advantage of a child's innocence. It is not disgraceful to keep a secret. It is disgraceful to burden a child with a harmful secret that must be kept.

October 9

Many people are working on the prevention of child sex abuse. Still, many children are sexually assaulted and molested each and every day. Victimization happens to girls and boys all around the world. Our silence is their silence. Children need to know that surviving sexual abuse is not the end of the world. They also need to know that when they become an adult, and the long-term effects of the abuse become most apparent, that there will be people who understand their pain. They will not have to wonder if it is appropriate to still talk about the abuse if we break the silence for them now. We are the models for healing. We do not have to allow one more generation of survivors to suffer from silence for 30 years like we did.

October 10

All of the "should have" and "could have" records that play in your head as you heal from childhood sexual abuse is likely from your adult mind trying to fit in with other, often wounded, adults.

Just remember that no adult survivor has to prove how strong they are by continuing to be around a person who violated them. Choosing to avoid the places where people who have violated you are also invited is not a sign of weakness. It is the weakness of a family, church or organization that refuses to stand up for what is right. They choose to create more space for violators than for those that they violated. We get to use our strength in the way that is most healing for us, not to make the family, church or organization look good. All you have to do is whatever is in your best healing interest.

October 11

To survive, we pay attention to all of the negativity around us. We notice every time someone steps out of line, and we rush to correct or reprimand them. As we heal, we turn attention inward. We notice the internal voice in our head that holds us back, voices that misinform us about ourselves and voices misinform us about others. We can transform our thoughts. If you think peace, harmony, joy and laughter to yourself a hundred times a day on a conscious level, there will be less time for the negative voices to speak up. Each time the slightest negative thought comes to your mind, repeat those words silently to yourself to slowly erase the focus on negative thoughts. This practice could change the way you see the world and the way the world sees you. Let the healing begin.

October 12

We can heal no one but ourselves. When we are ready to help others all we can do is create space for healing to occur. Believe it or not, the best way to help others is to be a living witness. I do not mean a "talking" witness, but a "living" witness. When you create a thriving life of your own, you show people that healing is possible. By doing so, you create space and energy for people around you to heal themselves.

October 13

In "error" to survive, many survivors overuse defense mechanisms. Survivors may see space as abandonment, questions as threats, balance as neglect, suggestions as insults, and the world looks and feels like a scary place. Healing requires us to pay attention to our interpretation of the world and our responses to other people's behavior toward us in an objective way. We must learn to challenge our minds, where our ego defenses live. We have to develop a sense of safety from within so that the world does not appear so scary.

October 14

Where did those feeling go? Betrayal, fear, powerlessness, guilt, shame, any or all of these feelings may have been a dominant part of our experience as survivors. To survive, however, we spend a lot of time suppressing negative feelings once we become adults. While suppressing feelings may allow us to function in the physical world, it does not heal our heart and mind. Suppressed feelings can become part of our world in unintended ways, such as perfectionism, irritability, hunger, lack of concentration, impatience or fatigue. These ways of being in the world are much more accepted flaws, so they take the place of the suppressed feelings. When we heal we return to a state of authenticity and deal with the real feelings, rather than the secondary ones.

October 15

Sometimes we look for big changes, and we miss all of the little ones. Sometimes we are so focused on the meaningless distractions that we miss the big picture. Sometimes we wait when we should be moving forward. Sometimes we expect a change in others that we should be making in ourselves. Sometimes we are too willing to blame ourselves instead of holding others accountable. Sometimes we try to push forward when the answer requires us to sit still. Sometimes we feel frustrated from all of the "sometimes."

OCTOBER 16

Not everything that goes wrong in your life is a result of childhood sexual abuse. In reality, adult life brings challenges to us all. However, everything that goes wrong in our adult life could trigger pain from the childhood sexual abuse. But the more we heal, the less likely we are to be triggered by the normal ups and downs of ordinary life. Every trigger of pain can move us further into our healing if we allow the connection to our past to happen fully. When life brings up the pain that is the best time to explore our past and heal our present.

OCTOBER 17

One long-term effect of surviving childhood sexual abuse is a denial of our sexuality. We deny our sexuality in three ways. Some survivors engage in sex carelessly to seek power or attention. They may frequently initiate sex to control their partners. Some survivors are too uncomfortable with sex to ever initiate. They continue to engage in sex only by demand and for the pleasure of another person. Other survivors maintain an unattractive appearance to avoid the invitation of sex altogether. They may intentionally carry extra weight, wear large clothing, dress in masculine clothing or neglect their physical appearance. Sex is never just sex for the survivor whether we choose to have it or not have it. We should pay attention to the decisions that we make about our sexuality, rather than deny it or exploit it. Healing can return us to a healthy balance and boundaries of sexual partnering. It is time to heal your sexual self.

October 18

Love, attachment and bonding are three different experiences of the human heart that people often confuse, particularly survivors. Love has no opposite because it is constant, unconditional and irrevocable. Love does not carry expectations with it. It is divine. It is not targeted and limited to one particular person. Many people never experience love, given or received, their entire life. Attachment is the intense experience of having a dependence on another person. Identities become intertwined, and you see the other person only as an extension of yourself. All of the person's behaviors are interpreted based on your needs. A specific person is often targeted for attachment, and you depend on that person to meet all or most of your emotional needs. The relationship revolves around expectations. When expectations are not met there is great pain or anger, and even confusion. Attachment frequently becomes confused with love and sometimes is the basis of abuse. There is also a fear of abandonment because abandonment is the opposite of attachment. Bonding is the emotional experience between two or more people who reflect each other's interests, emotional state, and desires. A connection is made at the heart level that supports desires to experience at least some aspects of life together. There are expectations, but not demands. There is the freedom to grow within the relationship as well as outside of the relationship, and even away from the relationship. Constant conflict, along with feelings of insecurity, may be a hint that your relationship is surviving on attachment rather than bonding or love. Attachments make us vulnerable to dysfunctional patterns of behavior in relationships.

October 19

When sexual assault grooming is done through admiration, the family is often the first target. The violator assures that he or she is embraced by the head of the family. The violator positions himself or herself to be needed and valued by the family by offering money, time or skills. The violator wants to make sure that the family depends on him or her. When the family depends on the violator so much that they could never see them as a bad person, only then may the grooming of the child begin. Imagine how easy this is when the violator is the breadwinner who pays the bills, or the perfect son who takes care of his little sister while the parents work, or the aunt who takes the children on summer vacation each year, the pastor who prays for the family, the neighbor who helps with home repairs or the coach who gives the child a ride home from practice. These are "the good guys" that society, parents and the legal system do not want to point a figure at, and neither does the child. In fact, the child often feels special, chosen, unique, loved or mature because he/she has the (warped) attention of such an admired person. The child has been "chosen" to have a "special" relationship. The family and the child are both victims of the violator. They both pay a hefty price for the attention of the violator.

October 20

There are healing problems, healing possibilities and, of course, healing progress. Where are you today? If you are not sure, then think about this. Healing does not require you to forgive the violator, but you also should not act angry toward the world. Healing does not require you to seek therapy, but you also should not try to heal others instead of yourself. Healing does not require you to participate in any religion, but you do not have to dismiss God. Healing does not require you to save humanity, but you also should not live selfishly. Healing does not require you to tell the world that you are a survivor, but you also should not be ashamed of being a survivor. Healing does not require you to say you are healed, but you should see some progress now and again. Try not to focus on the problems of heal, but the possibilities. You will experience progress.

October 21

We cannot change the past. However, we can explore it. Many circumstances surrounded our victimization of childhood sexual abuse including family dynamics, cultural and religious beliefs, and social systems. All of these systems contributed to our suffering, not just the physical invasion of the violator. Healing is an opportunity for us to review all of the people and systems involved. For example, violators rely on the silence of victims because dysfunctional families and organizations often breed silence. Whatever the reason we did not disclose as children, our silence was justified. Trust that! We did not create our vulnerability as children. We were likely isolated, neglected, raised in an unreasonably stressful environment or emotionally abandoned by care-givers. Our environment made us vulnerable to sexual abuse and its silence. We must heal from all of the dysfunction. If all we ever see is the physical acts associated with the abuse, then we will never fully understand or appreciate the significance of our survival. It is time to face the whole truth about all of our adverse childhood experiences that enabled the abuse.

October 22

Make sure that you do not continue to engage in sex with a victim mentality. You will struggle, needlessly, on the healing path if you do. The decision to have sex should not be based on someone making you feel insecure about the relationship. You should not have sex as a result of any threats or withholding of resources (such as money), and you should not be bullied into sex with insults or pouting. When you engage in sex under any of these circumstances, it is rape. Consensual sex can only occur if there is no coercion involved at all. Unfortunately, many survivors of childhood sexual abuse and incest end up in relationships where there is constant rape. Rape disempowers the victim in many ways, not just sexually. Some survivors are stuck on the path, not because of the past abuse, but because they remain in sexually abusive relationships. Resolving present abuse may be the key to healing the past.

October 23

You chose to read this book, which indicates that you are further along the healing path than the violator ever expected you to get. The violator and those who protect the violator have requested your silence in one way or another. You were supposed to forget about the abuse or pretend that it did not hurt you, or that what happened was normal. You were supposed to understand that no one meant to hurt you, or that the violators were once victims themselves, so you should not turn against them. You are supposed to see the positive change in the violator and erase memories of the past. You were never expected to gather support to reveal your truth. You were never supposed to speak of the horrors that time was supposed to make you forget. You were never supposed to become a light for others to find the healing path. You were not supposed to, but you did. Keep doing what you do.

October 24

Violators tend to hold victims responsible by using a variety of excuses like the victim was too beautiful to resist; they needed the victim; the victim did not say no, or the victim asked for it. These are the types of excuses that violators who groom their victims use in particular. In doing so, victims are seen by the violators as "partners." Of course, this eases their conscious. But as adult survivors, we have to identify sexual abuse for what it is. We were never partners. Violators do not have partners. They only have victims. Now we are survivors on the healing path. We will reject the lies and deceit and speak truth into our experience. We are victims no more.

October 25

Your right and need to heal from childhood sexual abuse does not depend on whether or not your abuse involved penetration. There is no such thing as a little sexual abuse. Penetration is not the only factor that matters. Age of initiation and discontinuation is important, the frequency of abuse is important, as well as the relationship between the victim and violator. Each case of abuse is different, but all sexual abuse is wrong and harmful.

October 26

Sometimes violators try to position themselves into the lives of their child victims once they become adults. Making contact is especially easy to do if the violator was the parent, sibling or some other significant family member. Avoiding contact with the violator is essential to healing because it can be a constant trigger for survivors. Often the survivor tries to leave gracefully without exposing the family shame. But the violator sometimes makes contact with the survivor via social media, phone calls or texting. You owe no one a compromise on healing no matter how they are related to you. You survived, and now you get to make all of the adult choices that you need to thrive. You can walk away without any explanation at all. You can deny a friend request, ignore a text, and decline invitations. You get to determine your actions based on your needs, not the needs of the violator! It is time to heal.

October 27

Survivors of childhood sexual abuse are vulnerable to revictimization in adulthood due to an impairment of social development. Distorted perceptions develop, and cause survivors to experience the world at face-value. Survivors tend to respond to whatever is immediately present without interpretation. We may perceive criticism as harsh and respond with a fear of abandonment. On the other hand, we may perceive attention as affirmation and respond with openness to vulnerability. Adults with healthy childhood development are not likely to respond to someone offering attention with openness to vulnerability. For example, a violator may offer compliments and gently touch women's arms and hands without permission within only minutes of meeting her. Most women with normal adult development would see this as invasive and turn away from the stranger who is crossing personal boundaries. Survivors with compromised social development are more likely to trust the person and admire their attention. By the time they realize the person's bad intention, the train may be coming too fast to get off of the track of re-victimization. Healing helps to repair our social cues to restore our defense mechanisms. When we learn how to be safe in the world, the world is a lot more fun.

October 28

Our brains are programmed to pay attention to salient features and ignore peripheral stimuli. What this means for survivors is that we tend to only focus on the sexual abuse as the cause of our mental/emotional health challenges. We tend to ignore conditions that surrounded the abuse. For example, the absence of a safety net means that even small mistakes have big consequences, which may decrease a child's desire to take responsible risks. On the other hand, having adult responsibilities as a child can create a willingness to take dangerous risks from having a sense of over-responsibility. Children in an overactive environment like criminal activity, constant conflict, unpredictable living arrangements or constant strangers in the house may have difficulty making decisions or forming stable relationships. A child who is often left alone may seek or accept attention from others at any cost. These types of situations can negatively influence how children learn to manage emotions. We have to explore our past in a comprehensive way to heal.

October 29

Remember that when we were children we had to hide a lot of pain, confusion and fear. We hid those feelings to fit in our environment, even though we still did not fit in. But there was nowhere else to go, so we just kept hiding and trying. It did not take long for us to start hiding from ourselves. That is how mind personas develop. Personas are conscious aspects of personality that serve a specific purpose for survival in a specific environment. Now that you are on the healing path you have to take back your life from your persona so that you can have a full life. Only your true self can live your true purpose.

October 30

Are you still carrying the secret instead of finding your voice? Are you still protecting your family reputation instead of healing? Doing so keeps you intimately tied to the violator. Keeping secrets and protecting is largely what defines intimacy. So even though you may not see the violator, you are still intimately tied as long as you are protecting the secret. The secret of sexual abuse was never yours to keep, no matter what you were told or how you were made to feel.

October 31

During the tender ages between three and six children's emotional development focuses on initiative. They learn to cooperate, especially with adults, and they learn to lead and follow. However, development can be interrupted or compromised by trauma. The development gap can lead to children remaining overly dependent on others. They may also become fearful of taking risks and less creative. Between the ages of six and twelve, child development focuses on building competence in children as they begin to understand rules and getting along with peers. Trauma at this age may development a sense of inferiority in a child instead of competence. Most childhood sexual abuse begins in one of these two phases. However, only a small portion of abuse is disclosed during these stages. The victim's development may remain compromised in adulthood. Even when their external behavior appears normal, the internal workings of the individual may continue to be distorted. However, the distortion may feel normal to the survivor because it is all that they know. The distortion becomes their world orientation and can manifest havoc in the social, physical or spiritual life the further the child survivor moves into adult life without dealing with the abuse. Fortunately, development never ends, so delayed adults who find the healing path can still fully develop. It is time to heal!

11: I AM

The death of a violator comes with a lot of emotion that most people do not understand. It changes us from the inside, especially those of us who lived our lives waiting to be chosen over them.

November 1

For most survivors the guilt and shame can only be combated with a lot of information. We have to understand the nature of childhood sexual abuse beyond our personal experience. You were only a single victim of a worldwide problem. You were never the problem. You have to know that the violator typically grooms victims. They prey on the emotional needs or immaturity of the child. If a child is lonely, the violator may offer attention. If a child is too restrained by parents, the violator may offer freedom through rebellion. If a child is neglected, the violator may offer "love." Of course, none of this is for the good of the victim, but strictly for the grooming of the victim to fulfill the violator's perverted interests. The immature mind of the child is also constricted by the dysfunction in the environment that makes safe space for the violator, but not the child. The reality of the child becomes distorted before a child can understand social relationships, appreciate authority or even value themselves as human beings. The illicit relationship sometimes becomes a strong identity of the child victim. You had no control over what arose in your environment, including the violator. You were a victim. Victims are under the control of bad people. So guilt and shame are just part of the distortion of reality from your past.

November 2

You have to go back a tiny bit further until you get to your true child nature, the nature of your vulnerability before you were introduced to the world of adult decisions. You have to connect to the confusion of chaos that happened in the home. That chaos led to isolation and emotional distress. No child can be blamed for how they develop under these conditions. No adult can be blamed for following the scripts that everyone told her was correct since childhood. We can trace the scripts back to their authors, and we can trace our beliefs back to our inner child and see the innocence as well. The connection is clear if you take a look at the evidence. We were innocent until made to feel guilty. Now we are slowly awakening.

November 3

Our knowledge of psychology, spirituality, loving and being loved is sometimes not enough knowing to remove the guilt and shame we carry. We shut down, shut out, act up and act out, trying to hold it all in and together. Many survivors choose denial and pretend like the experience of sexual abuse never existed. Denial is easier than addressing the ugliness that remains. However, you have spent enough years living in silence. You have spent enough time carrying the shame. Now it is time to open up so that you can heal. You are not alone.

November 4

It is possible to be afraid, but not stifled by the fear. It is possible to feel lonely, but not act out of anxiety. It is possible to feel rejected, but not compromise your self-interest. Feelings, good or bad, point us in a direction, but should not necessarily dictate our actions. Pay attention to what you feel, and then act deliberately, not desperately. Healing has begun.

November 5

It is more important that we accept our experiences than it is for anyone to apologize for the way they have treated us. It is more important that we forgive ourselves than it is for us to forgive anyone else. It is more important that we recognize our potential than it is for anyone to make us feel important. It is more important that we recognize the connection that we all share as human beings than it is for us to find a connection with one special person. It is also more important for us to create safe boundaries than it is to be able to trust someone. The point is to keep the focus within. If we place importance on external circumstances that we cannot control, then we give up too much personal power.

November 6

"Follow your heart" is a great concept to live by, but only if your heart is free from anger, fear, resentment, guilt and shame. If that negative energy is what fills your heart, then the choices that come from your heart may represent those negative emotions as well, and likely short change you in getting what your heart desires. If your heart is broken, and you follow the brokenness, then you are likely to end up in a broken space of life. First you have to "heal your heart." Then you can follow your heart.

November 7

Many times, survivors have people in their lives who want to help but have no idea how. Help with triggers is an invaluable way to support survivors. Supporters can be useful in helping to identify triggers as well as helping to recover from them. Survivors do not always know their triggers. Therefore, if a support person notices that there is an unwarranted shift in the survivor's mood they could inquire about it. If they see the shift on more than one occasion after similar events, the event is likely a trigger, whether the survivor knows it or not. It may be the presence of a particular person who looks similar to a violator, a particular song, TV scenes related to intimacy, or a common phrase related to the abuse, such as "you're so beautiful." All survivors have their triggers. Having someone who knows and understands them without judgment would be a big help.

November 8

Many of us have been told that we are somehow to blame or that the experience of abuse is insignificant. It is cruel to say that to an individual whose voice has been silenced. That statement is based on the person's fear of being alone, their avoidance of guilt about not protecting a child, the unwillingness to change, ignorance of child development, or a lack of awareness of the frequency of childhood sexual abuse. Their statements of blame are not based on truth. There are 60 million people that are alive today who are finally awakening from a world of silence, one by one. No one can tell them that their experiences are insignificant.

We will continue to put our voices together so that we can break the silence, so that the suffering can stop, so that we can heal.

November 9

Once you know the truth, you cannot turn away from it. However, just because you know the truth does not mean that you will put what you know to good use. Still, it is the knowing that gives us a choice. Some truths we have to know for a long time before we accumulate enough relevant experiences to fully practice what we know. But the knowing will help us pay attention to the experiences as they arise.

November 10

Survivors often feel like people in their life are doing them a favor regardless of the quality of the relationship. We end up partnering in friendships and intimate relationships out of fear or manipulation instead of reciprocal nurturing and caring. This often results in asking too much or expecting too little and placing ourselves in victim mode. The key is to practice self-love. You can show yourself kindness from looking in the mirror and telling yourself you are beautiful each day. You can tell yourself "I love you" as you explore your image. Until you can do these two basic tasks, it is nearly impossible to attract others who will do it for you.

November 11

Many survivors suffer from "mind chatter", the voices in the head that deliver negative messages on a constant basis, messages of fear, doubt and disempowerment. You are not enough, you are not significant, and you are not capable, so says the chatter. Then there are the constant messages about the world. It is scary, it is dangerous, it is bad, it is evil, and it is out to eat you alive. Chatter, chatter, chatter. The more you try to turn it off, the louder the noise gets. Do not try to stop the chatter, because that does not work. What does work over time is learning how to accept the chatter as chatter. Watch it as if you are watching a train go by on a track. Notice it and know that it is a part of who you are for now. There is no need to resist it. To resist it is to fight against yourself. But try to turn up the volume on the positive voices that often get drowned out by the chatter. That voice keeps telling you that tomorrow can be better. It keeps sending you to the websites to find understanding and knowledge about healing. It tells you to try what you have not tried before even though it is scary. That voice knows that there is still a lot of life to be lived, and you want to live it well. In other words, rather than fighting the mind chatter, just wake up your voice of faith, resilience, and hope. They are ready to speak, and when they do, they will begin to drown out the chatter more and more. Every time you hear the chatter, you should listen more closely to the voices of healing.

November 12

To find your inner strength, you have to be willing to see your weaknesses. Too often we look at the weaknesses of others to develop our strength. But criticizing and judging others cannot make us stronger, smarter, or more evolved. Sometimes the judgment of others helps us hide our weaknesses. When we keep our weaknesses hidden, we remain in darkness. We need to come out of darkness to heal. So, instead of using the judgment of others, we can use self-reflection to process our interactions. We can allow our reactions to arise from a level of consciousness rather than from our hyper-defensive mind. We could respond internally to our discomfort by pondering what person or situation triggered the uncomfortable reaction. Explore why you want a person in your life so badly that it hurts. Know what beliefs you are using to make judgments. Depending on the feedback loop, we can determine how we want to externally respond. You accept your initial reaction without judgment, introspect, then you choose your external response. Our engagement in this process empowers us to make decisions that move us forward.

November 13

Confrontation can be a painful experience if you are not prepared for the worst response from those you confront. It does not matter if you are confronting family members who knew or the violator. The negative responses to confrontation can throw a survivor for a big loop no matter how long the survivor has been on the healing path. If you are already challenged by a lack of memory, then having someone respond to you by insisting that your memory is incorrect could be devastating. If you are desperately in need of affirmation, then someone responding to your confrontation by ostracizing you from the group or by turning others against you can be even more devastating. If the response to confrontation is a physical threat or lawsuit, then that could throw you off the healing path. If you choose to confront, do so because you are powerful, not because you are needy.

November 14

Re-victimization occurs for about 50% of adult survivors of childhood sexual abuse. Even when the sexual abuse stops during childhood, we still are not safe. Unfortunately, many survivors stagnate at the age that they were when the abuse was initiated. The stagnation can happen at the brain level even though it is not related to intelligence. The survivor may be academically smart, but they may still view the world from a child's perspective. They may be challenged by complex interactions. For example, they may not speak up for themselves if they are confronted by someone. They may not be good at perceiving deception. They may blindly obey authority. A perpetrator capitalizes on these qualities in people and often target them. Please be clear that this post is not about trying to understand "deficits" of survivors. Survivors' "deficits" would not be deficits if the world would hold perpetrators accountable. This is about creating a safer world where people's vulnerabilities are protected by a larger loving community. It may start by breaking the silence of adult survivors of childhood sexual abuse. All of this mess that we keep bottled up inside with shame and guilt should be set free. We must say to survivors loud and clear that we believe you, and it was not your fault. Then we should point the finger at the bad guys who target people who trust them.

November 15

Honesty is the best policy when it comes to healing. Honesty with oneself is most important because you cannot be honest with others if you are not honest with yourself. You cannot be honest with yourself as long as your focus is on others. You have to turn your attention within to know your truth, to look at the obstacles that are created from within. How others treat you is a reflection of how you treat yourself. Be honest about how you treat yourself. Take a look at your fear of being alone, fear of rejection and your fear of not being enough and see how they force you into dysfunctional decisions about relationships that end in pain.

November 16

The decisions you make today define you much more than the trauma that happened to you as a child. What was done to us does not determine the level of healing we reach. Resilience happens in the mind, and it happens in the present moment to contribute to our fate. It starts with the beliefs we hold about our experience of the abuse. If you believe that everything was taken from you, then you have no reason to hold on or to fight. A person who is born blind does not spend their entire life wishing for sight. They focus more on the other senses that they have, rather than the one they do not have. Resilience means that we focus on what is empowering within us rather than what is absent or unavailable. Look past the void that keeps calling back your attention to your power. There is something beyond that beckons you to heal.

November 17

Our brain is supposed to help us to adapt to our environment. The brain does not know good or bad. It knows adaptation and survival. If sexual abuse is part of the environment, our brain will adapt to it. It is just that simple. Survivors develop an array of behavioral patterns to adapt to the abuse depending on the victim's brain. The only reason to explore our response to the sexual abuse is to better understand what needs to be healed. We should never reflect on our experience of abuse to determine if we are to blame in any way.

November 18

As your feelings about the abuse arise, keep the focus and conversation on yourself. Allow yourself to feel, for example, "I hate what he did to me." Give life to your feelings by going beyond the surface. Your mind was assaulted as well as your body. Survivors sometimes remember the physical acts of the abuse but forget about the grooming, trauma, and emotional betrayal. Remembering these aspects of the abuse could create a healthier response to the abuse. Explore your thoughts and feelings about your mental reactions to the abuse. Get in touch with that loss of power so that you can regain it. We have to know what we are healing from if we want to heal. We can only know by going within.

November 19

I can tell you lots of ways to find the strength to heal, but telling is not the way. You find strength with intention. Live daily with the intention to access your inner strength. Want it more than you want to be right. Needing to be right will keep you weak and closed in a box. Want it more than you want to be loved. Begging to be love will keep you focused on a void. Want it more than you want approval. Needing approval will keep you focused on the strength of others instead of your strength. In other words, let go of the wanting, and there you will find your strength.

November 20

Healing is a personal responsibility. No matter how much you try, you cannot shift it on to anyone else. Even though you 100% were not responsible for the abuse, you are 100% responsible for your healing. There is a belief that when someone hurts an innocent person deeply that there should be accountability, assistance, and acknowledgment. When survivors of childhood sexual abuse are offered these supports, they do heal faster. However, in most cases, no one is held accountable, no assistance is offered, and the abuse is not acknowledged. Nevertheless, we have the same personal responsibility to heal. We have to investigate, read, talk, risk, change, and grow. Time does not heal all wounds. Conscious healing heals all wounds.

November 21

Forgiveness does not require anyone to subject themselves to being mistreated by others. Fear does that. Survivors that carry an unconscious or conscious fear of abandonment sometimes choose to respond to their abuse with forgiveness rather than healing. They forgive so that they can stay in familiar relationships, even though the people they forgive have no change of heart or behavior. Forgiveness should not require you to lower your standards for relationships. Fear does that. Forgiveness does not beg for people to remain in your life. Fear does that. If forgiveness was a goal for you, then ask yourself what was the motivation. Look deep within to make sure your forgiveness does not come from a place of fear.

November 22

Attachment, past or present, to the violator, is one of the difficult challenges of healing. Accepting our attachment as a "survival behavior" rather than a flaw, stupidity, weakness or dirty is an important aspect of healing. Violators are the sick ones who are incapable of offering love without exploiting children. What you felt or feel for the violator is not genuine love, but manipulated compliance. Survivor's affinity toward the violator is like being at a magic show where you know that the woman was not sawed in half, but you sit in amazement at the magician's ability to make your eyes perceive that she was cut in half. No one leaves the show and goes home and try to cut someone in half. You know it was a trick, even if you do not know how it was performed. The same can be said for the love survivors feel for the violators. It is not real because it was all set up by the magician. The violator is the magician.

November 23

The pressure to forgive is an obstacle for survivors in the healing process. When survivors are told that forgiveness is required for healing, many would rather reject healing than forgive. They do not pursue any avenues of healing because they are not interested in forgiveness. Their lack of interest in forgiveness turns into a lack of interest in healing. We must stop spreading the untruth that forgiveness is the key to healing. Healing may lead to forgiveness, but forgiveness does not lead to healing. There are plenty of people who have forgiven the violator, yet still hate themselves. This is not healing. Some survivors who have forgiven the violator, cannot get along with anyone else. Their lives remain full of conflict. Healing is not about forgiveness of a particular person. Healing is finding a path to authentic living and transparency that bring you joy. You can be authentically you and angry at the same time. You can find positive ways to direct and transmute anger when you are authentically 'you' in being angry. There are not "bad" emotions. What you do with the energy of emotions leads to healthy living or not. There are many tasks and issues that will arise when we commit to healing. There is no order in which we will meet these tasks. Some people will make their journey about finding God and forgiveness. That is fine if it works for them. Others will make the journey about getting back into their bodies and focus on health and fitness. Other survivors will make the journey about restoring their close relationships and finding authentic love and commitment. As we journey together, we can create safe space for the paths that survivors walk without demanding or reprimanding. Safe space is full of love and acceptance.

November 24

Offering no resistance to healing is not a call to be passive in your life. It is just the opposite. No resistance follows natural physical laws of the universe. Think about what you should do if you are driving a car and you skid on ice. The worst reaction is to try to resist the skid. The safest maneuver is to steer your car into the skid and not slam on the brake. Novice drivers often do the opposite and create damage that could have been avoided. If someone pulls your hair you should never try to pull your head away to resist. The safest defense is to place your hand on theirs and press their hands into your head. If you find yourself falling, the safest response is to allow yourself to fall gracefully to the ground and break your fall with your arm. If you try to prevent the fall, you are more likely to end up twisting or breaking an ankle, causing more damage than a bruised arm. There are many examples related to physical safety that can help us understand the benefit of no resistance. We can be encouraged to trust the process on our healing journey as we learn what no resistance looks like in our personal lives.

November 25

Revisiting the past can be painful but is usually necessary to heal. Revisiting the past does not mean that we are going back to the past. What it means is that we are uncovering the pain that is present with us. The pain was created many years ago, but it has been present with us for a long time. We are now wading through the distractions and letting go of the defenses that hid the pain from the world and sometimes even from ourselves.

November 26

Hiding thoughts of suicide is one more secret that survivors carry. It is difficult to talk about and get people to understand the frequency in which some of us wish we were no longer here. The detachment we feel to life is unacceptable to people who do not understand the depth of our pain. We carry the thoughts and feelings in silent shame, pretending to care or faking interest in people, places, and events that are insignificant and irrelevant to healing. No matter how much the sun shines, it does not penetrate the shade of disappointment under which we live. No matter how much people love us, it does not expand to the depth of our self-hate. Look at us try one more day. Look at the resilience, the bravery, the perseverance within us even to live the way we do. There is a knowing in us that clings to life and keeps hope alive that we will find the key. Once we know, we know, no matter what our thoughts tell us. We will fly; we will soar. We must be here to fight another day so that we can make the world a better place. There is no shame in who we are or how we feel. There is only shame in a world that pretends to be perfect and insists that others pretend as well. Today, we choose life.

November 27

Incest is the terrible family secret, the skeleton in the closet and the horrifying clandestine family tradition. It is a real word, and it is a real experience. It is not our fault, our baggage, our burden or our shame. We were not participants in incest; we were the victims of it. Now we are the survivors. We are not the incest.

November 28

The end of November is a wicked time of year for many survivors. The next six weeks will be a challenge for most incest survivors. Incest is that ugly word that we too often minimize. But the holidays put it right in our face. Incest is the sexual abuse of a child who is victimized by any family member related by blood, marriage or by close living arrangements. So that includes, in-laws, cousins, the mother's boyfriends / father's girlfriends who live in the home, as well as grandparents and siblings. This is important to remember and understand when you get that ill feeling in your soul as you grapple with the holiday season. These are the people who are likely to be at the dinner table, and you are likely to shrink into victim mode unless you have a plan. Today is a good day to start thinking about how you will prepare for the holiday season, so it does not take you under.

November 29

Resistance cannot empower us. Acceptance is where we find our strength. Society, our families and friends, even our ego beckons us to "just let it go." We spend decades struggling with the concept of letting go. We try forgiveness. We adopt an attitude of perfectionism. We numb out with alcohol. We busy our lives with taking care of others. We even try to redo the perfect childhood by having children. We try one or more of these society-accepted tasks hoping that it will help us let go of our past, our pain, our trauma. We try it all, except acceptance. Acceptance is where empowering arises. When you allow the pain as if you had chosen it, you can own the pain instead of it owning you. When you cry without regret for the tears, mourn the loss of the innocence without shame, and express the hate without fear of going to hell, you take back your power. These empowering efforts require no resistance.

November 30

Healing progresses as you find your voice and begin to speak your truth. You do not need confirmation or affirmation. You should own your truth without apology. Speak to your significant other, children if they are old enough to understand, co-workers if you work at a safe place, and your friends if they are supportive. You do not need to give details to anyone. You can just state that you are a survivor and disclose the relationship of the violators if you want. "I was raped by my brother when I was seven years old, and now I'm finally trying to heal." That is how my disclosure went when I first broke my silence. Now I only state that I am an incest survivor and move on with the conversation without offering any detail. Practice with your one-liner just to hear yourself say it. If people ask questions that you do not want to address just let them know that you are still sorting through all of the years of silence right now and are not ready to talk about it yet. When you choose to live openly as a survivor being a survivor is public information, and details remain private. Living openly is a start to finding your voice.

12: THE KNOCK AT THE DOOR

There is no step by step process, but rather, a journey that awaits you. Remember, it is not a destination that you seek, it is internal peace. Now pay attention to what is inside of you.

December 1

The healing path is not a straight or flat road. There are layers to the journey. The layers do not come in a particular order, and we sometimes revisit layers. We can have layers close together or spread apart in time. Layers hide one another, so survivors tend not to know what is ahead of them. The layers make healing challenging because sometimes we believe that we are further along than we are. We forget that we are on a journey that lasts a lifetime, and we start to feel like we have arrived when life is going well. Then, out of nowhere, it seems, another layer of healing is revealed. It beckons us to move forward. Some of the layers include coming further out of denial, deciding when and how to disclose, exploring all of the adverse childhood experiences related to the abuse, letting go of dysfunctional people and patterns, and learning to trust the healing process. Something triggers you to move to the next level. Lean in gracefully and gratefully.

December 2

One of the ways our mind holds our emotions hostage is through dichotomous thinking. Dichotomous thinking is the pattern of making conclusions of opposites. Any behavior that does not match what is right in your mind is automatically seen as wrong. For example, if you post on social media and people who are close to you do not click "Like," you conclude that they "do not like." If someone does not say, "I love you" every time you say it, you conclude that they do not love you. If someone does not call you back right away, you assume they do not want to talk to you. This type of strict interpretation of behavior may create conflict in relationships. Understanding other people's perspective can be challenging for survivors who are stuck with dichotomous thinking. The good news is that we can change our brains over time with the practice not reacting. Give yourself a moment to feel your internal reaction, and then process it by asking yourself if you are experiencing dichotomous thinking.

December 3

Your inner child cannot be free as long as you continue to sacrifice your body for the pleasure of intimate partners. Your relationship with your partner should not mimic, in any way, the forced interaction with the violators. In healthy relationships, the partner makes sure that the other partner is fully satisfied. They do not allow or request their partners to frequently offer their body without experiencing pleasure. Sex is a natural and healthy human experience, and it should feel healthy. There should not be any shame attached to consensual sex. You can do more harm to your inner child than any good you think you are doing to your relationship with your partner by sacrificing your body. Sex is too deeply connected to emotional, physical, and mental health to be ignored.

December 4

Many survivors are filled with anger and rage. That is often easier than admitting self-hate and shame. Anger is energy that can be used for good but is often negatively applied because too often we are told and taught to not be angry. For many of us, anger may be just what we need to move forward. Anger is a response that directs us to look at a situation and look within. However, many survivors do not let those feelings in, and the anger is misdirected. Misdirected anger causes more damage. We can give new life to the anger and use it for transformation. Transformative anger can propel a survivor forward. Survivors may transform anger into art, activism, ideas or creativity. When a survivors transforms the anger, sexual abuse may not be represented at all in what gets created. The anger may transform into art, sports, science or entrepreneurship. The transformation may open up a whole new world for the survivor with a new platform for healing.

December 5

Drug addiction is an obvious defense mechanism for survivors of trauma. However, the use of drugs is so common that the addiction part may be missed for a long time. It serves as a viable defense mechanism to allow the survivor to remain in denial for a long time. Since drug addiction works so well for so long, recovering is extremely difficult, no matter what the drug of choice is. Nevertheless, many people do end up recovering, either on their own or with self-help groups or professional help. However, many people who recover from the addiction remain in denial of the need to heal from the childhood trauma. Many remain in emotional pain for their entire lives. Being sober, or dry is not the same as being healed. We must adequately address our issues of childhood sexual abuse to experience peace.

December 6

Make healing "wholistic." Instead of seeking to heal from childhood sexual abuse, look at the bigger picture. Even people who have not had our particular experience need healing. The world needs healing. Every human being collects baggage that prevents them from living fully. Our baggage is heavy, but it is still just baggage, rather than who we are. But healing is a commitment no matter what the baggage. Seek information and support for healing the world and you might find some of what has been missing in your healing practices.

December 7

Some survivors use denial to avoid embarrassment. The fear of embarrassment has kept a lot of people miserable. It keeps people in bad marriages, causes people to lie about their status, and makes many people conform to ideas that they do not believe. It also prevents many people from living openly as a survivor. But, accepting the identity of the survivor as an experience, rather than a statement of being, can release the fear of embarrassment that may keep us stuck in other areas of our lives. While we are living in denial, we tend to make choices that keep us stuck rather than move us forward. We may subject ourselves to careers we do not like, partners who do not respect us and friends who do not value us. As we heal, we come to see many of our choices for what they were, part of our denial. As we heal, we give ourselves permission to assess these choices without embarrassment. But first we have to completely let go of the embarrassment of being a survivor and all of the issues that have entered our adult lives as a result of the experience.

December 8

There is one healing path with infinite diversions. You can make the choices that best fit you. Consider your financial resources marital status, your children's ages and your own. Consider where you live, your physical limitations, your employment, and employability. These are just some of the variables that affect your life every day that you cannot change overnight, if at all. They influence your healing journey. They influence the choices that are available to you, the path you take and how fast you can go on it. While we should learn from others, we should not compare our healing journey to others. We should not try to follow anyone's book, program or theory exactly as it worked for someone else. All information that we encounter about the healing path is just pointers, guidance, or a reference. Information is key, but it is not "the key" to healing. You are the key, your willingness to risk, your faith in the process and your determination to act upon the information that greets you on the path based on your personal situation.

December 9

Anger can be a difficult emotion to sort through because the threat (that created the anger) is no longer present. The moment to strike anger seems long gone. It is difficult to capture the right to be angry without hurting oneself or others. If the anger is directed inward, then a survivor may use coping mechanisms of self-harm, including starvation, addiction, cutting, or sabotage. The world may not notice the survivor's destructive patterns because they are often hidden. If the anger is directed outward, then the survivor may become, unfaithful, confrontational, or rebellious. The person themselves may not notice the destructive patterns because other people may seem to be the cause of reactions. Rather than directing anger inward or outward, anger must be transmuted into useful or divine beauty.

December 10

A pretty smile can hide the ugliest pain, and a great job can be the biggest distraction from the internal work of healing. Laughter with good friends can disguise the tears of betrayal from those who were initially responsible for your care. A slim body frame never shows the heavy weight of the burden you carry from keeping a secret that was never yours to keep. A life of exotic travel can cover up your inability to be still. Who knows of your sleepless nights, abuse of medication and drugs, self-harm, troubled thoughts, broken relationships, and your fear and anxiety? You have tried to fix yourself or hide. You have tried everything except living openly to let the wound breathe and heal. It is time to heal.

December 11

This holiday season give yourself the gift of healing. Give yourself permission to not spend time with the people who violated you and those who support them. Give yourself permission to not explain your absence from family functions. Give yourself permission to tell your children the truth about the family you grew up in as an incest survivor. Give yourself permission to find support for your healing. Your ideal of a happy home is as mythical as Santa Clause as long as the home is where the violator is. Give yourself permission to choose who you call family.

December 12

Tis the season… often for depression, grief, and regret, as well as feeling abandoned, feeling unappreciated, feeling pressured to please. Pay extra attention to yourself over the next month. Pamper yourself. Thrown away old scripts that box you into a corner of trying to please others or stay in their good graces. You do not have to visit anyone you do not want to genuinely spend time with or buy gifts for anyone. You are on the healing path, not the path to popularity.

December 13

The average survivor is violated by three perpetrators before the age of eighteen. In some cases, multiple violators may have presented to the child during the same period. But what often happens is that there are three or more periods of sexual abuse before the age of eighteen. The abuse usually occurs on and off by different violators. Usually, the child is in a dysfunctional home environment that does not provide for children to develop skills to protect their personal boundaries. Moreover, if a family has one violator in it, it is likely to have another. The "family" might be a biological family unit, a church family, school family or any other unit that is supposed to operate in the best interest of the child but exploits children instead. Adult survivors who have multiple victimizations experience a lot of shame because they do not realize that multiple victimizations is so common. It has nothing to do with the victim's choices.

December 14

Being in the world is where you test how far you are in your healing. Often, we need to withdrawal from the world to gather our strength and collect ourselves. But isolating is not the same as healing. There are many more risks to take, but we should become better at predicting the outcomes, especially as we address our tendency to experience "mind-blindness." Life always brings us opportunity to practice that which we have not yet mastered. Do not stop living amongst the living. Live boldly, heal boldly.

December 15

By now we know there is a connection between what the mind feels and what the body chooses to experience. The opposite is true as well and can work to our advantage. If emotional pain elicits a desire to harm the body, caring for the body can elicit emotional peace. We can help heal the mind through caring for the body. We can start by looking in the mirror and accepting all that is reflected back at us. We can commit to eating nutritiously, meditating and exercising. We can rest the body with soothing vacations and caress the body with calming baths. What we do with and to our bodies matters in significant ways. Use it to heal.

December 16

In research, there is a phrase that says, "Correlation is not causation." Just because two events happen at the same time does not mean that one event caused the other event to happen. It only means that there is some "relationship" between the two events. We should not assume that the experience of childhood sexual abuse "causes" all of our problems. The fact is that there is only a "relationship" between childhood sexual abuse and our problems, but the relationship is not "causal." This understanding makes a difference. If we believe childhood sexual abuse causes depression, anxiety, social awkwardness, and low self-esteem, then we are doomed because the cause has been placed in effect. Every survivor would have the same problems caused by the abuse. The reason survivors do not all have the same adult problems is because childhood sexual abuse does not "cause" any of the problems in adulthood. It is only "related" to the problems that we have. We must do exploratory work from within to understand the relationship between our childhood and adult experiences. This is what the healing journey is about and why it lasts a lifetime. We weaken the relationship between our past and our present experiences. When we do so, we can have reasonably satisfying lives.

December 17

Forgotten memories that finally break through to the conscious level do so for a reason. Try not to fight the memories, because you are likely to miss the message that is coded within the memory. Recovering lost memories is part of the healing process that includes recovering lost pain. It all comes up to be healed when you are strong enough to use it to heal. Memories are not there to harm you but to heal you. Try to embrace them. The goal is not to get rid of the memory because the way our mind works, the more we try to suppress a thought of behavior, the more drawn we are to acting on it. The goal is to allow the memories to exist within us without taking us under. You may need help to explore the memories, Eye Movement Desensitization and Reprocessing (EMDR) could help. Running can have a similar effect as EMDR (but cannot replace professional help if you need it). Decide what you need to help you get through the memories, but acknowledge them as a healing tool.

December 18

You can tell your story a thousand times, and the pain will not subside. Childhood sexual abuse is not a fairy tale with a happy ending. We heal when we work through the experience of trauma. Learning to recite a story of sexual abuse is like learning the

ABCs. You have to know your alphabet to learn how to read. However, learning the alphabet does not teach you how to read at all. We learn how to read by understanding the intricate relationship between letters, then words, and if we study the language we can become master writers, not just readers. Do not focus on building a story. Focus on understanding the experience of childhood sexual abuse and your personal experience of resilience. Study the language of healing. Practice the art of healing. Share the joy of healing.

December 19

Childhood sexual abuse is not a single incident for most victims. It is an experience that begins before the violator ever touches the child and lasts long after the last touch. Most victims are targeted based on specific factors such as isolation, family conflict, developmental delay or prior experience with abuse. The average violator targets dozens of children, not just one, even though each victim may believe that they are the only one. Victims often live with violators around them, eating at the same table, praying in church together, driving home together, helping with their homework assignments or playing with them. A prior relationship exists between the violator and victim in 90% of cases. The child has no room to resist. Resistance is not a choice when violators target children no more than you can stop the storm from flooding your house. However, the child survived. You are a survivor now, no matter how many years you remained in the relationship with violators. It is healing time, time to create an experience of healing. Healing is not a single incident either. It is an experience, but this experience, you must choose.

December 20

As we grow into adulthood, we tend to view the experience of the childhood abuse from a grown-up perspective. The adult voice in your head tends to punish the child within. This conflict is often what is going on when you blame yourself for the abuse. You are blaming your inner child, the person you were during the abuse. You refuse to see yourself as helpless, so you blame the child. In this time, you must remember that children have no schema for the scheme of betrayal. You cannot blame a child for failing to act rationally in an irrational situation. The child had only one responsibility, survive! Now you must learn to thrive.

December 21

This healing journey is as much neurological as it is psychological. The structure of your brain changes as healing occurs. You can change the structure with prescription drugs if necessary, and for many this is the necessary way. But for many survivors, there are less intrusive ways to change the structure of the brain. We can change the brain with nutrition and exercise or meditation practices. But the structure of your brain must change. Parts that are over-active must calm down, and parts that are under-responsive must become engaged. This journey will not progress much by just reading a few daily affirmations although daily affirmations are a great beginning that can lead you to do the work on yourself. Talk therapy is useful to the degree that it motivates you to invest in life-changes that improve your brain. The more active you are in working to change your brain, the more likely your brain is to change. Use the tools that are available to you and that you can commit to using regularly. You have to be actively involved in the process.

December 22

There is a difference between confrontation and disclosure. When we confront someone our aim is to let them know that we are hurt or disappointed or frustrated as a result of their past behavior. We do not necessarily demand any change, apology or other gesture from the person. Sometimes we confront to let the person know that we will change our behavior toward them rather than us requesting that they change their behavior toward us. This is sometimes the case when survivors go "no contact" (although we can go NC without any communication about it). When we disclose, we simply let someone know about our experience. We can disclose to anyone for a number of reasons, and we can disclose as little or a much as we want on any given account of disclosure. But disclosure can be just as damaging as confrontations, no matter how little or how much we disclose.

December 23

How do you know who to trust? That is an external question. To answer that question, you would have to investigate every single person you come into contact with, and you would still have misjudgments. However, if we make questions internal, we may get better results. How can I learn to trust myself so that I am not so vulnerable to abuse? That question only requires us to investigate one person. Questions that may help you investigate self may include what was I looking for that allowed me to give up control so readily? What will letting go of this relationship teach me about myself? What am I afraid of feeling when I am without a partner? What will holding onto this relationship teach me about myself? Am I looking for a reason for this person to stay or looking for a reason to let them go? Internal questions move us forward, not just ease our mind. When we focus on the behavior of others, we may ease our mind, but rarely do we move forward. Healing often requires us to do that which is most difficult to do to get to a place that is easy to be.

December 24

Mind-blindness interferes greatly with our ability to predict our own and other's behavior. When we live with mind-blindness, we are like the horses with the blinders on the side of their face. All they can see is what is right ahead of them. They move forward without any consideration of what is around them. As humans, life is too complex to move through with blinders. To successfully navigate our interactions, we need a panoramic view. We need to be able to string together a series of events that have led to the present moment to successfully predict the near future. For example, if someone is only pleasant when they are in need, you have to be able to string together all the events in which that person is pleasant to respond appropriately. On the other hand, if someone is always there for you when you need them, but does not call you as much as you think they should, then you also have to be able to string together those events instead of responding negatively based on your need to feel special through constant attention. The ability to predict your happiness based on your interaction with people, combined with the responsibility for self is a good sign that you are not experiencing mind-blindness. If you are not there yet, then remember that healing is a journey, and you may get there sooner than you think.

December 25

On Christmas Day, many of us will make the most important decision yet on our healing path. Will you do what you have always done, which is make yourself small to fit into someone else's space, or will you stand up for yourself? There are many ways to stand up for yourself that do not necessarily involve confrontation, but it does require making choices. You can accept dinner with a friend instead of having dinner with the violator and their supporters. You can volunteer at a homeless shelter. You can plan a vacation out of the state. You can take someone with you to dinner to serve as a buffer or pull you away if the environment gets too rocky for you. You can deliver gifts the night before or the day after. You do not have to jump into a confrontation to set yourself free. There can be many baby steps along the way, like avoiding being in the presence of violators and their supporters.

December 26

For all the bad choices, painful emotions, useless investments of our time, have no regrets. A life without risk is not a life well spent. None of us knows what any day will bring. Every yesterday brought us to this exact moment. Every moment is an opportunity to choose what you were too afraid to choose before, to risk what you did not want to risk before, to grab what you thought you could not hold onto, to love yourself like you did not know you could be loved.

December 27

Healing hurts, but it does not all hurt. The first time you stood up for yourself felt good. There were also times that you self-disclosed and the person told you they are a survivor too, and your heart felt lighter. You feel less afraid in life now that you have faced your biggest fear of living openly. You have met friends on the healing path, and you now know that you are not crazy. You got a life makeover just because you were brave. Healing makes us better people.

December 28

Being survivors of childhood sexual abuse and incest means we are resilient. But it also means the patterns that developed our resilience may be the same patterns that get in our way. We have learned to live successfully in this world despite our negative experiences. We have learned to bounce back from pain. We have learned to give more when we thought we did not have anything left to give. We have learned to predict what people need and ignore our needs so that we can stay in the game. We have learned to walk away with our head up and move on when we cannot get what we need. All of these survival patterns have contributed to our resilience. Unfortunately, resilience is not inner peace. To move toward inner peace, we have to learn inner stillness, which is much more difficult than resilience. Many people are naturally resilient, but most people have to work hard at inner stillness because to achieve inner stillness we have to unlearn most of what we learned to become resilient.

December 29

The approach that you take to healing depends on where you are right now. Do you know how the abuse is manifesting itself in your life at this moment? Many support groups do not discuss the actual acts of abuse because that is the only part that we can never change. But how we approach life as a result of the abuse is the daily challenge. How do you relate to yourself? What are the messages that you give yourself about who you are and who others are? What exactly do you need to heal to heal from the abuse? How is the abuse getting in your way? Memories of the abuse take on a life of their own that will change as you heal. Our perceptions of the past may even change as we heal. The focus of the healing is in the present, where the changes can do us the most good.

December 30

The silence that survivors of childhood sexual abuse and incest experience is not that quiet space of peace and tranquility that one seeks after a long day of work. It is not that comfortable silence that sweeps over the room after the baby finally stops crying and drifts off to sleep. It is not the sweet silence of flirtation when just a glance is enough to capture your interest. There is gentle silence, and there is LOUD SILENCE like the secrets of incest. This silence is like the silencer on a gun so that no one knows someone has been murdered. It is like the nightmare silence that prevents you from screaming in your dream of being captured by the beast. It is the like the silent gasp of disbelief when a person is given a terminal diagnosis. Like a court-imposed gag order, many survivors live in the silent spaces where pain echoes off the walls of the empty room. The only way to break the silence is to leave the room. Walk through the front door, sneak out the back door, climb out the window or go up the chimney. Just leave.

December 31

When you commit to the healing path, you commit to change, and you do not get to choose how your life will change. That is why we say "Trust the process." Healing means that you will be in a better place than where you started. But this only happens through change and difficult transformation. Cancer survivors have to endure chemotherapy, a patient with a broken bone has to endure six weeks in a cast, and a person doing house restoration often endures financial depletion. Healing and restoration must occur at the deepest level. The most basic structure must become stabilized. Healing tools must penetrate through whatever is covering the structure. For survivors, that means some relationships will fade out. Some jobs will end. Some marriages will dissolve, and some organization memberships will be terminated. Ideas will turn over, and thoughts will turn around. Inaction will become action and action will become stillness. Try not to resist the change. Welcome the new you.

ABOUT THE AUTHOR

The woman in me is seven years old
She cries because her story has never been told
Everyone loved her, but no one loved her quite enough
She was the baby of the family, but she had to grow up tough
Carrying the weight of siblings and parents on her shoulders
She manifested in 1962, but her spirit was definitely much older

Life as a seven-year-old ain't all that bad
Her sense of humor always reminds me to laugh
Her laugh is hardy and loud, so loud it is contagious
She can take your heart to some sentimental places
Like the day she met her father, and he picked her up in his arms
For seven years she'd waited for him to right this wrong
She never found out why he left before she was born
But having him come back made her heart warm
Until he put a Bible in her hand and broke every commandment
Every Sunday in church she asked God to help her understand it
Why was her life so full of contradiction
Dysfunctional dissonance, lies and friction

Why was the cost of being loved so high
She learned love was a trap that could never satisfy
So rather than feeling, she began to think outside of
*   the box*
She learned to be slyer than the fox
Better to give than to receive... bullshit
She made sure to take whatever she could get
She looked out for number one
Didn't let the day end without the job getting done
Her heart and head were in constant conflict
Because her heart yearned for love, but her head was
*   too thick*
She carries more baggage than Santa on Christmas Eve
But she ain't carrying gifts; her bags are full of fear
*   and need*
She occasionally makes an attempt to grow up
But the pain in her life just keeps her stuck

But being stuck at seven ain't all bad
I sometimes find pieces of childhood that I never had
I take my dog to the playground so I can swing on the
*   swings*
Curiosity and adventure are the wind beneath my wings
I run so that age can't catch up with me
I dance to show the world that my body is now free

She sleeps like a baby because she works hard, and plays
*   all day*
She calls upon magic when she loses her way
She uses her words to let our story unfold
To release the secrets that weren't supposed to be told
Pandora's Box hidden in my skeleton closet
Her silence wasn't bought with a wallet
And the can of worms she carries ain't for fishing

It's the horror of clandestine family tradition

The only way to grow up is to grow away from childish scripts
But the healing journey is a long emotional trip
Sometimes I just rest a spell and chat with my seven-year-old self
Because that's what's good for my emotional health
I live with her with no regrets
She survived the experiences I've tried to forget
She is the woman in me
She is the little girl that set me free
She is me

www.ingramcontent.com/pod-product-compliance
Lightning Source LLC
Chambersburg PA
CBHW061321040426
42444CB00011B/2723